Machine Embroidery

Machine Embroidery

INSPIRATIONAL QUILTING TECHNIQUES

JENNY HASKINS

AUSSIE PUBLISHERS

Dedicated to two exceptional men in my life. To my son Simon who is a kindred spirit and knows how I feel, sometimes before I do, and to Daryl Craze who is my balance and is admired by all in the industry. With thanks, love and admiration.

AUSSIE PUBLISHERS
25–27 Izett Street
Prahran
Victoria, Australia 3181
Web site: http://www.penguin-threads.com.au

First published by Aussie Publishers 1998
10 9 8 7 6 5 4 3 2 1

Created and produced by The Watermark Press, Sydney
Text copyright © Jenny Haskins 1998
Machine embroidery and project designs copyright © Jenny Haskins 1998
This compilation copyright © Aussie Publishers 1998

Editor: Diane Wallis
Designer: Cathy Campbell
Photography: Simon Blackall
Styling: Jenny Haskins
Printed and bound by L. Rex Printing Co Ltd., China

National Library of Australia
Cataloguing-in-Publication Data

Haskins, Jenny.
Machine Embroidery : inspirational quilting techniques

ISBN 1 876364 05 X

1. Embroidery, Machine. I. Title.

746.44028

Contents

Introduction

*O*ver the past seven years I have designed and made seven original quilts. Three of them – *The Heritage Quilt*, *Field of Dreams* and *The Colour Purple* – were developed as tools for teaching machine embroidery classes. During the course students would create a quilt, block by block, and at the year's end a prize was awarded for the best quilt. I was, and still am, humbled by the raw talent (so far in advance of anything I possess) which was exhibited in the resulting quilts.

This reminds me of the story of British athlete Roger Bannister who was the first man to break the four minute mile. For years no-one could break this barrier, but once Roger showed that it could be done, others achieved the same goal in quick succession. Whenever we reach beyond ourselves, we open the door for others to follow.

If you are familiar with my other publications (*Victorian Dreams*, *The Colour Purple* and *Amadeus)* you will realize I am a romantic at heart and love movies with a message. This book is no exception. *Arsenic and Old Lace*, which is how I describe the colours and mood of all the projects in this publication, is the name of a golden oldie starring an all time favourite actor, Cary Grant. It is a deceptive movie; nothing is as it seems on the surface. We are pre-conditioned to hear the word 'lavender' with 'old lace' which always conjures up a sweet, old-fashioned mood, but 'arsenic' is the surprise substitution. And so it is with the technique which is common to all projects in this book. Everything is not as it appears to be. It may look difficult, but it is really easy and fun to do.

The *Arsenic and Old Lace* quilt was inspired by a new range of thread colours. Such was the impact of these new colours that I barely left my workroom and hardly slept for ten days (colours affect me like this), but at the end of that time I had my quilt finished.

That was two years ago and during this time, two other books were published. The *Arsenic and Old Lace* technique and quilt proved to be very popular and scored a close second to *The Heritage Quilt* in requests for printed instructions which flowed into my workroom. Since finishing the *Arsenic and Old Lace* quilt I 're-opened the file' and embellished it further for this book. A project such as this is well suited to bursts and lulls of enthusiasm and activity. Although it appears to be a huge undertaking, do not be afraid to accept the challenge because you can add to the quilt as your skills develop. You can even use this technique on an existing store bought quilt and not sew at all if you wish. But the rewards of a project such as this are far greater when you call on your own creativity.

While working on the concept of this book, I decided to expand the theme to include the furnishings for a whole bedroom which is centred on the quilt, plus an enchanting vest for good measure. Like *The Colour Purple*, the techniques revealed here can be applied to many other projects; I only touch on a few. You can start in a small way by making a cushion, a wall hanging or just a vest. Make my projects at first, then develop your own. The sky is the limit. I am only taking you to the edge; you have your own wings and can 'soar with the eagles'.

Auntie Mame, (in the movie of the same name) tells Patrick (her nephew) 'Patrick, oh my Patrick, life is a banquet and most poor fools are sitting round starving'. The banquet is set – you are my guests, rejoice in your own creativity.

Basic Equipment

Whenever you embark on any project, knowledge, preparation and skills are necessary in order to complete it successfully. However, there is no substitute for practice, patience and perseverance. Along with these 'three Ps' having a wonderful sewing machine and knowing how to use it as well as using the right threads, needles, fabric and accessories will smooth the path of endeavour to your finished work of art.

However, if you do not sew or only have basic stitching skills and an equally basic sewing machine, you can make a very acceptable version of the *Arsenic and Old Lace* quilt. The simplest way is just to fix ribbons, laces and doilies to an existing plain quilt using the recommended techniques of bonding with heat from an iron. Or you could construct the blocks (with or without sewing) and then join them with machine stitching. It is up to you, your resources and the skills you wish to acquire.

Because all projects use the equipment listed below, make sure you are properly equipped for the job before you begin.

Basic equipment, from top in a meandering clockwise direction: embroidery sewing machine, rotary cutter (yellow handle), self-healing cutting mat, Pellon (iron-on batting/fusible fleece), strip of Vliesofix/Wonderunder (fusible web), reducing glass (larger, clear), quilting pins (long with bead heads), shading glass, open-toed embroidery foot, darning foot/big foot, marking pen — one end water soluble (blue), the other end fading (purple), Madeira pre-wound bobbin, 1000 metre reels of Madeira Rayon 40, Madeira Monofil, Audrey's Bond Powder, tape measure, transparent plastic ruler, ribbons, dressmaking scissors.

SEWING MACHINE

I have a top of the range sewing/embroidery machine which I purchased when I left a sewing machine company and I can make it do anything. The effects seen in the projects in this book are achieved by stitch building, free motion machine embroidery, quilting, applique and embroidery designs. If you do not have a top of the range embroidery machine, you may wish to purchase additional lacey motifs from a fabric store or specialist haberdasher to use as substitutes for machine embroidery. With a basic model sewing machine you can outline quilt or use free motion embroidery to achieve effects which are similar to mine.

Needles

Use an 80/90 large eyed embroidery sewing machine needle because this needle has a bigger eye than normal to allow for thread expansion due to friction and thus prevents breaking/shedding of thread.

Feet

An open-toed embroidery foot is used for all guided machine embroidery such as applique, stitch building

Darning foot/big foot, for free motion machine work such as thread painting, outline quilting and stipple quilting.

Walking foot – an accessory on all machines except the Pfaff which incorporates a compact built-in walking foot (dual feed). The walking foot is perfect for all forms of sewing/embroidery but is especially good for quilting or any form of fabric layering as it ensures perfect sewing/piecing at all times. With a walking foot, the top and bottom layers are fed equally into the path of the needle to avoid the top layer being stretched out of alignment with the bottom. You may wish to purchase a walking foot if you do not have one.

Over edge foot is particularly useful when you want to 'stitch in the ditch' to secure

Open-toed embroidery foot holds a broad area of fabric taut during machine embroidery.

Darning foot/big foot is used here for stipple quilting.

Walking foot – this one is an attachment which is clipped on when desired.

Over edge foot gives accurate guidance when you want to stitch in a 'ditch' which has been made by a previous seam or row of stitching.

Couching foot has a guide through which threads, ribbons or braids can be fed into the path of the needle.

the top layer to the bottom through an existing stitch line. The guide ensures that a line of new stitching is exactly over the previous line.

Couching foot is designed to guide one or more threads, braids or ribbon into the path of the needle where they can be stitched (couched) down with embroidery stitches. Stitches curved lines with ease.

Threads

(Or in other words, texture and colour) – I always use Madeira thread for its colour, texture and reliability.

Madeira 80 denier Cotona – for free motion stipple quilting.

Madeira Monofilament – transparent thread for attaching lace and outline quilting.

Madeira Rayon 40 – 40 denier embroidery thread for machine embroidery and applique.

Bobbin thread

Pre-wound bobbins by Madeira have one third more than Bobbinfil and are ready to use. Simply insert one in the bobbin case, as is. The threads are held together with a bonding product; nothing is left when the bobbin is finished. Pre-wound bobbins also activate the bobbin monitor when low.

Stabilizers

These hold fabric stable when machine embroidering so the fabric won't pucker. There are many forms, but I used 'Stick it all' a tear away stabilizer that self adheres to the back of the fabric, and tears away afterward.

SEWING BASKET ESSENTIALS

Rotary cutter and mat – Ideal for multi-piece straight edge cutting.

Quilting ruler – easy to use, transparent and clearly marked.

Purple or blue marking pens – Blue is water-soluble, purple fades over time.

Vliesofix / Wonderunder – double sided fusible web, bonds fabric with heat and prevents fabric edges fraying when cutting.

Audrey's Bond Powder – This is a permanent heat bonding agent which is ideal for applying motifs and lace. Wonderful for quilt backs when quilting through.

Applique mat – When heat bonding it protects fabric and absorbs glue substances from bonding agents.

Quilting pins – extra long fine pins with glass bead heads.

Reducing glass – optically reduces your work to a miniature of its actual size enabling you to see the overall effect. Useful, particularly, for gauging 'gaps' and imbalances in a design as a whole.

Shading glass – optically emphasizes the intensity of colour values by reducing everything to a monotone.

Iron on fleece (wadding) or Pellon – iron on quilt batting. H640 from Freudenburg.

Dressmaking scissors

Tracing paper

Unpicker/seam ripper – electric versions such as Peggy's Stitch Eraser are also available which allow you to clip and remove unwanted stitching in a matter of seconds.

Quality iron – an industrial strength continuous steam iron will ensure perfect pressing and steaming on your machine embroidery, and vertical steaming for finished quilts

Non-slip ironing board cover – new on the market, it's ideal for all your ironing and craft needs as the surface holds the fabric firmly and prevents it from slipping.

Blue flexible curve – although not strictly an essential, this apparatus is useful if you have difficulty drawing swags free hand.

TIP

When changing thread, clip the thread close to the thread reel and pull your thread through the tension in the direction it would normally pass. This prevents any lint or shredded thread from being caught in the tension discs. The same procedure can be applied to the bobbin.

Tips, tricks and techniques

Decorative work done on a sewing machine is considered to be machine embellishment or embroidery. One of my machine embroidered quilts includes fabric layering, piecing, thread painting and machine embroidery. With careful planning, a little help from your imagination, great thread, fabric and colour coordination, you too can create a superlative set of soft furnishings for the bedroom. Below are listed the techniques used in conjunction with the above to give you a head start.

MACHINE EMBROIDERY/EMBELLISHMENT

The use of machine stitches to enhance your work can be either an extension of a design or part of it. In a single row or multiple rows called stitch building, machine embroidery can be the main feature or used in association with applique or quilting.

FREE MOTION

This involves lowering your feed dogs, tightening your lower tension and loosening your upper tension to between 2 and 3. Attach a free motion embroidery foot such as a darning foot/big foot and select a straight or zigzag stitch. Engage your tension, you can then guide the fabric in any direction as the feed dogs are lowered and no longer feed the fabric. The artist determines the length and density of the stitching. This takes practice so make sure you do plenty before you start on your project. There are three main classes of free motion work.

Machine Thread Painting

When thread painting it is important to use a fast machine and slow hands. Follow the lines and directions of your design to define and highlight the colours as in hand embroidery. This can be done over a design, as a new design or over a soluble stabilizer in a hoop to create a free standing design.

Free Motion — Outline Quilting

This is usually done using a transparent thread such as Monofil or in a matching thread colour to the background fabric and outlines designs or motifs to define and quilt them. It is also used to attach such elements as lace and motifs.

Free Motion — Stipple Quilting

Using a darning foot/big foot that gives clear vision with either a matching 80 denier thread or Monofil, quilt through all layers of fabric using a modified figure eight meandering stitch design — the lines of this design never touch or cross one another.

Four examples of stipple quilting. The stitching line meanders like the course of an old riverbed.

APPLIQUE

This involves applying a fabric shape, motif, ribbon, lace, or doily onto a background of another fabric. The fabric/lace that is to be appliqued has a fusible web such as Vliesofix/Wonderunder ironed onto the back of it to allow it to be heat bonded to the background, as well as preventing raw edges fraying. The bonded element is further enhanced by having its edges covered with machine embroidery stitches. Rather than use a plain satin stitch, I prefer to use machine embroidery stitches that are satin stitch based such as a scallop, a triangle and a curve to enhance my work. Take this a step further with stitch building adding lace- and scallop-type stitches to the edge of the original row of stitches.

DOILY/LACE BONDING

The easiest and cheapest way to do this is to use the Audrey's Bond Powder. Determine the placement of your doily and I usually do a rough drawing with fading marking pen around the piece that is to be bonded. Lightly sprinkle a little bonding powder in this area as you would salt. Place your doily over this then cover it with an applique mat and press in place using a hot dry iron. Any excess powder will be picked up by the applique mat and can be easily wiped off before next use. One tin of powder goes a long way and is much cheaper than double sided webs.

QUILTING THROUGH WITH AUDREY'S BOND POWDER

When the quilt is pieced, cut the quilt backing up to 5 cm (2 in) larger on all four sides than the actual quilt. Before applying the quilt backing, place quilt front right side down on the ironing board, batting facing up. Lightly sprinkle Audrey's Bond Powder onto the batting, place quilt backing over batting making sure you centre it and press in place with a hot iron. Work your way down the quilt ensuring the fabric is square and even. The bonding powder lightly fuses the quilt backing to the batting so that you can quilt though with ease, eliminating the need to pin. Should the fabric move, a light press with a steam iron will re-bond it.

QUILT BINDING

Cut your quilt binding fabric either on the straight or bias according to your preference. As the binding is folded in half lengthwise before it is stitched, allow a generous width, say around 10 cm (4 in).

Bias Binding

Cut your fabric on the bias remembering to allow for 6 mm (¼ in) seams and the centre lengthwise fold. Join your bias pieces in one continuous strip, always joining them on the straight grain of the fabric in order to avoid a bubbled seam (but the join will however be at a 45° angle to the edge of the strip). Iron this strip in half lengthwise, with right sides and raw edges together.

Cut the strips of Vliesofix no more than 2.5 cm (1 in) wide. Iron this (paper side uppermost) to the edge of the bias strip so that it sits exactly on the folded edge; this will now be the wrong side of the quilt binding. DO NOT PEEL PAPER FROM BACK OF VLIESOFIX AS THE STICKY SURFACE REVEALED MAY PROVE TO BE A NUISANCE AS YOU MACHINE STITCH.

Round the corners of your quilt with scissors firstly marking out an arc with a fading marking pen on each of the four corners so the bias binding will curve easily. On the right side of the quilt with the wrong side (with Vliesofix) of binding facing up, match raw edges of bias binding with raw edge of quilt. Allowing a 6 mm (¼ in) seam, attach with a straight stitch.

Join binding by turning under the raw edges of one end of the bias strip and slipping the other end into the fold; seam through all

1. *Fold calico (muslin) square on diagonal into a double thickness triangle. Bias is on long side. Fold long side in half. With rotary cutter on mat cut into four-thickness strips.*

2. *Place two bias strips at right angles. The line drawn between the widest meeting points of strips is your seam line. Join with straight stitch. Trim seam allowance.*

3. *Fold strip in half lengthwise with their wrong sides together and their raw edges matching, and press with a steam iron.*

4. *Iron Vliesofix / Wonderunder strip to bias binding with edge on folded edge of calico (muslin). Do not remove the paper from Vliesofix / Wonderunder. This is underside of binding.*

5. *Pin binding strip to quilt edge; right sides together, raw edges matching. With straight stitch, sew binding to quilt edge. Pull away paper, turn binding over to wrong side of quilt.*

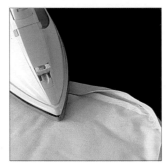

6. *Press binding in place; four straight sides first, corners last. Then ease in curve with fingers just prior to pressing with the iron. Will hold permanently without stitching.*

layers. Now you can peel the paper from the back of the strip of Vliesofix. Fold binding over to the wrong side of the quilt so that the folded edge (with the Vliesofix residue beneath it) just covers the row of stitching just completed. Press in place, working on all four straight sides first and leaving the corners until last.

Then ease in the curve with your fingers just prior to pressing with the iron. This will hold permanently without any stitching, especially if you have plenty of heat and steam in your iron. If not and you do wish to 'stitch in the ditch' from the right side, do so with a transparent thread in the needle and an opaque thread in a colour to match the backing in the bobbin.

Straight Binding

Straight binding is attached in four separate pieces; two opposite sides first and then the top and bottom.

Again cut your fabric (but on the straight grain) to suit your needs and seam allowance as above. Join if necessary. You will need the length to be at least 7.5 cm (3 in) longer than each side. Fold binding strip in half lengthwise as above, and iron 2.5 cm (1 in) strip of Vliesofix to the folded edge of the binding. Again, DO NOT PEEL PAPER FROM BACK OF VLIESOFIX. Attach with straight stitch on opposite sides of the quilt as above, and remove paper. Fold binding over to the wrong side and iron in place. Trim binding ends level the quilt.

For the top and bottom, work again from the right side and centre binding strips with raw edges and right sides together. There will be 3.5 cm (1½ in) overhangs at the side edges; fold these to the back and pin in place. Attach binding as before with straight stitch seams. Fold binding up and bond only the overhang pieces to the binding with an iron and then iron a small patch of Vliesofix to the folded edge of the binding on each end of the quilt. Fold over the binding strip as before and press it in place. Again you may choose to 'stitch in the ditch' from the right side to finish, but it is not necessary.

QUILT HANGERS

These can be in the form of three to four small loops of fabric about 5 cm (2 in) wide, or as a continuous pocket, or as ties. All serve the same purpose which is to display a quilt on a wall by hanging it from a rod. I have used all three systems and their means of hanging are incorporated with the binding on the wrong side of the quilt. The raw edges of the loops, pocket or ties are matched to the raw edges of the quilt and binding. You can anchor the hangers to the top of the binding so the quilt hangs in a straight line. This can be done by hand or machine.

After centring cardboard template on the Pellon backed block by matching horizontal and vertical lines, draw around the template with a blue marking pen. This squares up each block and marks the seam line in the one action. Pin blocks together matching these lines, and you get a perfect result every time.

JOINING QUILTED BLOCKS

When you are quilting as you go, this means each block is quilted and embroidered individually (and in the case of the *Arsenic and Old Lace* quilt, quilted through again when the project is pieced). Remember that embroidery and quilting will shrink the blocks, so make sure you allow for this. When blocks have been completed, make a cardboard template the size that you wish the blocks to be when joined (finished size). Mark this to divide it both vertically and horizontally across the centre. Mark each block on the Pellon side in the same manner. Now place the template over the back of the block and matching centre marks on each side (centring template) draw around the template with a blue pen. This squares up each block and marks the seam line in one action. Pin blocks together matching these lines, and you get a perfect result every time.

EMBROIDERED MOTIFS

With today's technology it is possible to have machine embroidered motifs that rival those of multi head, commercial embroidery machines in complexity and finish. The size, quality and diversity of designs available is still a source of amazement to me.

These motifs come on a design card or you can choose your own designs from a catalogue and make up a personal design card. Add to this the possibility of a Windows driven software program designed for domestic sewing machines. This program allows you to design your own motifs, automatically digitize them, then, via an interface cable, send them to your machine to stitch out.

The Internet is another valuable source for the machine embroiderer with thousands of designs which can be accessed by pressing a key. All these designs are stitched out in a hoop. For perfect stitching and accurate placement, use a hoop designed to stitch embroidered motifs on base ball caps called a Hoop-it-all with Stick-it-all paper. Choose the size and direction of your design first, then place the fabric under the needle to determine exactly where you want your design to be stitched. Remove fabric from machine then press its wrong side to the sticky backing stabilizer so that it is smooth and taut and stitch out your design.

When the design is finished, tear away backing paper. This technique eliminates the need for an extra fabric layer to compensate for the tension exerted on the work when it is placed in a hoop.

The hoop and paper can also be used on a finished garment to embroider cuffs and collars with ease. I used this method for all my motif embroidery designs. (Design software and the Hoop-it-all are made for all brands of machines.)

STITCH BUILDING

By starting with a single row of decorative machine stitching and then adding to it with a mirror reverse row of the same stitching or even something quite different, a delightful result is achieved that is greater that the sum of its parts.

Some stitches are best suited to applique while others seem destined for a lace effect. To enhance a design element such as a heart, I may outline the edge with a satin stitched scallop and then add a row of delicate filigree with curlicues and scrolls a centimetre (⅜ in) beyond the scallops.

Remember to stitch build with an eye to balance. Too many rows of solid stitches together could result in a heavy look whilst too many wispy ones may appear indistinct or fail to attract attention at all.

Match the stitches I have used to those that resemble them as closely as possible on your sewing machine.

GLOSSARY OF STITCHES

Because of advances in technology over the last couple of decades, domestic sewing machines have reached previously undreamed-of levels of sophistication. Today, a top of the range domestic embroidery machine can stitch out motifs which, not so long ago, could only have been achieved with a multi head industrial machine. It is also possible to use built in stitches to achieve amazing effects.

In stores, at demonstrations and craft shows I have often heard onlookers say 'I own a machine just like that, but I don't know how to use it or what to do with it'. How disappointing this is to hear. After all when you invest in a sewing machine you should use it. Don't be intimidated by the technology; it is easy to make it work for you.

The *Arsenic and Old Lace* quilt is an intriguing project which will reveal what your machine can do as you progress from block to block. Each block uses different stitches with altered width, length and density; you'll be amazed by the wonderful effects that can be achieved by simply stitch building. Not only does this teach you stitch combinations and effects, it also teaches you how to use you machine and how to get the very best out of it.

At the right are listed the stitches I have used in the *Arsenic and Old Lace* projects. Use the list as a guide, matching your machine stitches as closely as possible to those I have used if you want to produce a replica of my original. Please do not be limited in any way by my stitch choices.

TIP

I use photocopy paper at the back of my work when doing machine embroidery which acts as a stabilizer. When the piece you are working on is finished simply tear excess paper away, before going on to the next step.

Applique Stitches

# st. 1.	L 8.0	W 6.0	den .25
# st. 2.	L 10.0	W 6.0	den .25
# st. 3.	L 10.0	W 6.0	den .25
# st. 4.	L 4 - 6	W 4 - 6	den .25
# st. 5.	L 6.0	W 8.0	
# st. 6.	L .25	W 7.5	
# st. 7.	L 10.0	W 6.0	den .25
# st. 8.	L 10.0	W 6.0	den .25
# st. 9.	L 35	W 8.0	
# st. 10.	L 30	W 7.5	
# st. 11.	L 25	W 8.0	
# st. 12.	L 10.0	W 6.0	den .25
# st. 13.	L 6.0	W 6.0	den .25

Edge Stitches

# st. 14	SL 16	W 9.0	
	CL 12.	W 8.0	
# st. 15.	L 10.0	W 6.0	
# st. 16.	L 12	W 9.0	
# st. 17.	L 40	W 8.0	
# st. 18.	L 8.0	W 9.0	
# st. 19.	L 12.0	W 7.5	

KEY TO STITCHES		
L = length	den = density	C = curved edges
W = width	S = straight edges	

Scallop Edges

# st. 20.	L 10.0	W 6.0	den .25
# st. 21.	L 10.0	W 7.0	den .25
# st. 22.	L 12.0	W 7.0	
# st. 23.	L 10.0	W 6.0	den .25

Couching Stitches

# st. 24.	L 4.0	W 8.0
# st. 25.	L 6.0	W 6.0
# st. 26.	L 3.0	W 3.0
# st. 27.	L 25	W 8.0
# st. 28.	L 25	W 9.0
# st. 29.	L 12.0	W 9.0

ANTIQUE TEA DYE

You don't have to use cream doilies exclusively for antique-looking results. White doilies are often more plentiful and cheaper than cream and they can be dyed to a more mellow shade. Use this simple process on new fabric to give it an aged look. I include the coffee because there are times when tea alone gives fabric a rather pink tinge.

Ingredients: 2 tablespoons of instant coffee, 2 tea bags, 2 tablespoons of vinegar, 2 litres boiling water Wet doilies/lace in hot water first, then immerse totally in the dye bath. You can even boil them in the microwave for a couple of minutes, then rinse in cold water. Remember they will dry to be one shade lighter. Repeat the process if the colour is not dark enough. Make allowance for different fibres and fabric types; colour and density may vary, so test first.

Colour and Design

*M*any years ago I was fortunate enough to attend a lecture by a wonderful artist named Jean Saddler who shared her ideas and revealed her amazing talents with ease. She dealt only with colour and design, explaining that no matter how good you are at any art form, your achievements will be limited unless you understand design and can work with colour.

This is so true. Think about what it is that attracts you to something. Whether we realise it or not, it is the design and colour. Our attention is attracted by the way a work flows and holds the eye captive and by the way the colours work together as a whole.

When I talk with fellow artists there is unanimous agreement that the most crucial time in the course of any project is that which is spent on choosing the colours, matching and playing with fabrics and the gradual development of the design.

Colour sense is a gift and if you do not have it then you must follow the rules. There are many books published which explain how colour works, but a rule of thumb for choosing compatible colours is to ensure that they all have the same value (the white [tint] or black [shade] content determining lightness or darkness) and to repeat a common colour throughout your design to tie it all together. An imbalance of colour value is why some combinations are destined to failure such as a softly greyed pastel being swamped and discredited by an intense pure colour. But put the same pastel with companions of similar value that exhibit misty, cloudy qualities and the effect can be superb.

It is also useful to look at a colour wheel; a circular representation of the spectrum. Outside the optical laboratory, the spectrum can be glimpsed in nature in the form of a rainbow where light hits tiny droplets of water and we see the resulting colours of the rainbow ranging from red to violet through orange, yellow, green and blue.

The red, yellow and blue are pure (primary) colours and cannot be created by mixing. The orange, green and violet are secondary colours and are achieved by mixtures of primaries on either side of them.

Right: Assembling threads and fabrics for a project.
Left: Starting from the top, and working clockwise.
Rayon 40 by Madeira: 1082 Pale Cream (at 12 o'clock), 1084 Dark Cream, 1142 Mushroom, 1060 Silver Grey, 1306 Silver Green, 1055 Light Golden Brown, 1126 Dark Golden Brown, 1053 Apricot, 1054 Dark Apricot. Monofilament (transparent thread) is in the centre with a pre-wound bobbin on top.
Not shown: 504 Cream Tanne 50 denier for quilting. 504 Cream Tanne 30 denier for construction.
These thread colours determine the colour scheme for all the Arsenic and Old Lace projects and in the instructions are referred to by number alone. Refer back to these when choosing coloured ribbon and lace. Any extra thread colours used are identified by number and colour. Remember that 1000 metre reels of thread are the most convenient to use and the most economical.

The colour wheel gives a simple view of primary, secondary and tertiary colours, their contrasts (opposites or complements) and harmonies (neighbours). Cool green, blue and violet are grouped together on one side of the wheel with the warm reds, oranges and yellows on the other.

In a twelve part colour wheel, there are six additional 'wedges' of tertiary colour, one between each primary and secondary colour, and these are the results of a mix of a primary and its closest secondary colour.

But the colour wheel only takes in the tiniest fraction of the colours we are capable of seeing, estimated to be up to 10 million. Imagine lots of concentric circles starting at the centre of the wheel and working out to its circumference with the innermost being black and the outermost white with a carefully graded progression of these neutrals in between. In the very middle of the black and white bands would be a circular strip of pure or saturated colours.

The wonder of the colour wheel is that it enables us to gauge how colours will harmonise, how to find their opposites (contrasts or complements), how to distinguish those that are cool and those that are warm. Contrasting (complementary) colours are directly opposite one another on the colour wheel; red's complement is green, yellow's complement is violet and blue's complement is orange. The contrasts to the tertiary colours are also positioned as opposites on the colour wheel while the harmonies to all twelve colours abut one another. The wheel also groups the cool greens, blues and violets in one half the warm reds, oranges and yellows in the other.

The colour wheel may appear to be a rather academic and soulless tool to some people but its value is that even those with an unerring natural talent can benefit by delving into colour theory and thereby become acquainted, even in a rudimentary way, with the science of colour.

Design can be taught, and if practised long enough, then becomes second nature to you. I remember when the wonders of the lazy 'S' came into my life as a graceful graphic means of linking design elements. I also thrill to the use of odd numbers of the same or similar shapes or rows of stitching and the division of a component of a quilt block (or the quilt block as a whole) into thirds. Another favourite method of 'travelling' across a space is the use of interlocking curved lines. Once these means and methods are familiar to you, you will have the ability to design with ease.

Design is not very mysterious. It is basically straight lines and curves, squares, triangles and circles, ovals, half and quarter circles which flow onto curved lazy lines.

I start by drawing up my designs roughly, and work from there. A few changes are usually made to the original, but the drawing is a good reference point. Then I lay out the components, grouping my fabrics, threads and embellishments together and live with them

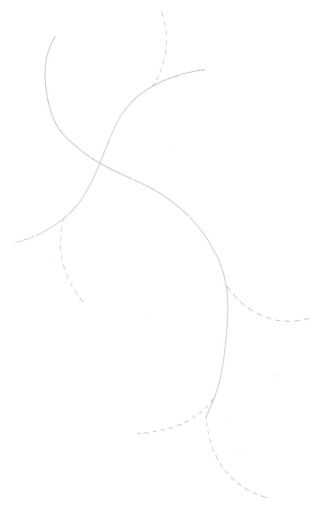

The most pleasing design line is the lazy 'S' which can be built on with ease (see broken lines in diagram), and you can be assured that the finished creation will work.

for a while before making the design permanent. This really gives me a chance to see how everything works together.

In the early stages, ask other people what they think. You don't have to take their advice but outside opinions can give you a different direction and a fresh view of the project.

When creating a design remember that there is always an easy way to interpret it in the finished article (see Tips, Tricks and Techniques on page 12).

Today, we are frequently limited by what we are told we can't do. If you are one of those who think your destiny is to follow a set design exactly because you can't draw, my reply is that everyone can draw to varying degrees of expertise but still draw. Just loosen the wrist, relax the grip on the pen or pencil and have a go. I guarantee you'll surprise yourself.

When selecting thread colours and fabrics, less is best. Always work with no more than five different coloured threads in one project. The repetition of these colours will ensure that your work is unified. If you are not sure about selecting colours, use just one coloured thread and repeat it in every design to tie your work together.

Your design should flow easily and yet be connected. The most pleasing design line is the lazy 'S' which can be built on, and you can be assured that the finished creation will work well.

When putting your project together, use reducing and shading glasses to help you acquire the right balance and combination of colours to ensure the overall effect will be pleasing. Seeing 'gaps' in a design miniaturised by a reducing glass is very enlightening.

Do not restrict yourself merely to the ideas shown in this book; the techniques and applications are limited only by your imagination. My role is to open the door to your total creative freedom.

Frilled Cushions

Have you ever wanted to do something really creative with those hand worked doilies you've inherited? I have found a way to solve your dilemma with a project that marries the beauty of handwork and magic of computer driven machine embroidery. This is a great place to start. Learn the technique as you make the cushion and you finish up with a wonderful decorating accessory as well.

NOTE

I have used calico (muslin) for the quilted projects in this book but contrary to most instructions in quilting books, I never pre-shrink it by machine washing it in hot water prior to sewing. By the time it has been bonded to Pellon (fusible fleece/iron-on batting) and stitched through with embellishments and quilting, a square is slightly reduced in size anyway. Once washed, although it may shrink slightly, I find that ironing with a good quality steam iron restores the item to pretty much its original size.

MATERIALS

- Two 38 cm (15 in) squares iron-on Pellon for both cushions
- 2 m (2 yd) 150 cm (60 in) wide unbleached calico (muslin) for cushion and frill for both cushions
- Two 13 cm (5 in) diameter doilies for cushion 1
- 18 cm (7 in) diameter Battenburg lace doily for cushion 2
- 30 cm × 10 cm (12 in × 4 in) cotton edging lace for cushion 2
- 1 m (1 yd) of 5 cm (2 in) wide apricot satin ribbon for both cushions
- 81 cm (32 in) of 5 cm (2 in) wide coffee satin ribbon for both cushions
- 10 cm (4 in) apricot fabric for applique for cushion 1
- 20 cm (8 in) Vliesofix (Wonderunder)
- 1 applique mat
- Madeira Rayon 40 embroidery threads in colours 1053, 1060, 1055 and 1084
- Madeira Monofil
- 80/90 large eyed needle
- Blue water fading pen, pins, scissors, tape measure, photocopy paper

PREPARATION

BOTH CUSHIONS

Cut two 38 cm (15 in) squares of calico and fuse matching Pellon square to the back. Iron Vliesofix to the back of the apricot fabric, all ribbons, lace and doilies. Cut apricot fabric into two 10 cm (4 in) squares.

CUSHION 1

Cut one 13 cm (5 in) doily in half. Place one coffee and one apricot ribbon strip across opposite corners of the cushion front, 13 cm (5 in) from each corner, place raw edges of half doilies under ribbon pieces. Iron in place, using applique mat. Pin second doily in place.

CUSHION 2

Iron an apricot and a coffee ribbon strip (apricot closest to the corner) abutting one another across one corner. Place lace across opposite corner with an apricot ribbon strip over its straight edge. Iron in place. Then pin the circular Battenburg doily in place.

BOTH CUSHIONS

Using a blue water fading pen, sketch in bow loops and tails as per photograph as well as positions for applique and embroidery.

•••••••••• NOTE ••••••••••

The lily applique can be added to with sprays of machine embroidery in # st. 2. Make the three lines curve a little and reduce the size of the stitch at the end of each line.

••••••••••••••••••••••••••••••

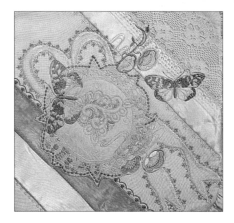

•••••••••• NOTE ••••••••••

Refer to the patterns of bow loops and tails on page 58 if you feel that drawing them freehand straight onto the fabric is too challenging. Change the proportions and positions of the loops and tails to suit your design.

••••••••••••••••••••••••••••••

METHOD

CUSHION 1

1. Stitch the doily pieces in place with small straight stitch and matching thread, following the doily shape.

2. Embroidery sequence: Apricot ribbon – matching thread st. # 9. Coffee ribbon – matching thread st. # 3 plus st. # 16.

3. Iron remaining circular doily in place overlapping ribbons by 2 cm (¾ in). Stitch in place.

4. Embroider bow loops and tails with cream thread using st. # 6 and silver grey thread for lace edge st. # 14.

5. Either using traditional applique, or machine embroidery, applique apricot lilies (see pattern below) in place on either side of the doily so that they overlap ribbons, using silver grey thread.

6. Select cream thread and another embroidery motif. Embroider in place.

CUSHION 2

1. Stitch scalloped edge of lace down with matching thread and small straight stitch.

2. Apricot ribbon (overlapping lace) is stitched with matching thread in st. # 12, outside st. # 14.

3. Apricot ribbon (on opposite corner) has its corner edge stitched with matching thread in st. # 5.

4. Stitch coffee ribbon with silver grey thread st. # 6, golden brown thread st. # 22.

5. Iron Battenburg doily in place. Applique doily down following doily shape with light golden brown thread st. # 4.

6. Embroider bow loops and tails as per cushion 2.

7. Matching thread colours and embroidery designs to the photograph, finish off with embroidery motifs.

MAKING UP

1. Cut strips of calico 20 cm (8 in) wide for the frill and join into one strip twice the diameter of cushion. Fold lengthwise and join ends, right sides and raw edges together. Gather this loop along its cut edge to fit the cushion front. Attach the frill to the outside of the cushion with right sides and raw edges together and folded edge of frill angled towards the centre of the cushion front.

2. Cut two pieces of calico 25 cm x 38 cm (10 in x 15 in) for the cushion back. Hem one 38 cm (15 in) edge on each piece. Overlap the hemmed edges to make a square that matches the cushion front and place over the cushion front/frill assembly with right sides and raw edges together.

3. Stitch around all sides. Clip, trim, turn to right side through slit in back and fill with cushion insert. Repeat for second cushion.

LILY MOTIF
Work this versatile lily motif in any direction.

Arsenic and Old Lace Quilt

You do not have to be clever to create this quilt, just smart. People say that in order to be successful at anything you have to work very hard. I do not disagree entirely with this and I always work hard, but the adage 'Don't work harder just smarter' also makes good sense to me. This project endorses this saying; as always it is not clever, just smart.

NOTE

Instructions are for finished quilt size of 160 cm x 214 cm (63 in x 84 in) which fits a single bed. The easiest way to increase the size for a double, queen or king size bed, is to make the centre block wider, adding another two Battenburg doilies with bow loops and tails (bow loops pointing to the centre) on either side of the apricot ribbon-swagged central motif. With space considerably expanded between the doily/bow embellishments, some additional appliques could be added before the background is free motion stipple quilted. With this extra width, you will also need more blocks across the top and bottom.

MATERIALS

- ☐ 7 m (7¾ yd) unbleached calico (muslin) 150 cm (60 in) wide for quilt front, back, sashing and binding
- ☐ 5 m (5½ yd) iron-on Pellon H415 (fusible fleece) for blocks, sashing and centre
- ☐ 2 m (80 in) Vliesofix (Wonderunder) for ribbons, centre applique and binding
- ☐ 8.5 m (9 yd) apricot satin piping for inside quilt binding
- ☐ 1 m (1 yd) apricot fabric to match thread colour for centre swag and appliques.

LACE AND BRAID

- ☐ 10 m (11 yd) butterfly edging lace 10 cm (4 in) wide for outside edge of quilt
- ☐ 80 cm (32 in) cream tatted edging lace 2.5 cm (1 in) wide for either narrow side of centre design
- ☐ 4 circular medallions 5 cm (2 in) diameter for bow centres on sashing
- ☐ 2 m (2 yd) cream cotton edging lace 7.5 cm (3 in) wide for centre block
- ☐ 51 cm (20 in) cream cotton straight sided lace 2.5 cm (1 in) wide for centre block
- ☐ 1.45 m (56 in) cream satin braid 1.5 cm (½ in) wide for centre block.

DOILIES

- ☐ 4 square doilies 15 cm (6 in) for corners of centre ribbon swag
- ☐ 3 square Battenburg doilies 18 cm (7 in), one for quilt centre, two for blocks
- ☐ 4 circular Battenburg doilies 20 cm (8 in) diameter, two for centre, two for blocks

- ☐ 10 circular crocheted doilies 18 cm (7 in) diameter for eleven blocks
- ☐ 4 small circular lace doilies 12.5 cm (5 in) diameter for four blocks
- ☐ Circular crocheted doily 30.5 cm (12 in) diameter for one block.

RIBBONS

- ☐ 75 cm (30 in) apricot satin ribbon 5 cm (2 in) wide for centre and one block
- ☐ 1.5 m (60 in) apricot satin ribbon 4 cm (1½ in) wide for two blocks
- ☐ 2 m (2 yd) apricot satin ribbon 3 mm (⅛ in) wide for threading in doilies
- ☐ 1.5 m (60 in) coffee satin ribbon 5 cm (2 in) wide for centre and five blocks
- ☐ 70 cm (28 in) coffee taffeta ribbon 4 cm (1½ in) wide for two blocks
- ☐ 2 m (2 yd) coffee satin ribbon 3 mm (⅛ in) wide for threading in doilies
- ☐ 2.5 m (3 yd) grey green satin ribbon 2.5 cm (1 in) wide for six blocks
- ☐ 2 m (2 yd) grey green satin ribbon 3 mm (⅛ in) wide for threading in doilies
- ☐ 50 cm (20 in) pale cream satin ribbon 6 mm (¼ in) wide for threading in doilies.

THREADS

- ☐ Madeira Rayon 40 embroidery thread (1000 m reels) one in each of the following colours 1082, 1084, 1142, 1060, 1306, 1055, 1126, 1053, and 1054
- ☐ 1 reel of 1000 m Madeira

Tanne 50 denier cream thread for quilting
- ☐ 1 reel of 1000 m Madeira Tanne 30 denier cream thread for construction
- ☐ 1 reel Madeira Monofil
- ☐ Pre-wound bobbins
- ☐ 10 bobbins wound with Madeira Tanne 50 for free motion stipple work and outline quilting
- ☐ Couching thread in small amounts in silver (block 9) and apricot, coffee and gold (block 20) for decorative effects. Couching foot guides thread to the needle's path where it is attached to the fabric with decorative machine stitching.

MACHINE

- ☐ FEET Open toe, zipper, free motion (big foot/darning), couching
- ☐ NEEDLES 80/90 large eyed embroidery
- ☐ EMBROIDERY CARDS of butterflies, flowers and cross stitch or bought motifs that best match those used in the quilt.

MISCELLANEOUS

Large glass bead headed quilting pins, blue/purple marking pens, quilting ruler, Olfa mat and rotary cutter, large dress making scissors, small sharp scissors, Hoop-it-all, Stick-it-all backing stabilizer, photocopy paper for stabilizing, one tin Audrey's Bond Powder, reducing and shading glasses.

PREPARATION

CALICO (MUSLIN)

Cut the following

- [ ] 20 blocks 30 cm (12 in) square to give finished size 27 cm (10¾ in)
- [ ] 1 block 137 cm × 83 cm (54 in × 32 in) for finished size 81 cm (32 in for centre)
- [ ] 2 strips 214 cm × 12 cm (84 in × 4¾ in) for finished size 209 cm × 10 cm (4 in × 83 in) for long sides of sashing
- [ ] 2 strips measuring 137 cm × 12 cm (54 in × 4¾ in) for finished size 135 cm × 10 cm (53 in × 4 in) for short sides of sashing
- [ ] Strips cut on the bias joined together (see page 000) to measure 8 m (8½ yd) long and 12.5 cm (5 in) wide, folded in half length wise to measure 6.25 cm (2½ in) for quilt binding.

Remaining fabric will be used for quilt backing and cut to suit the finished project.

PELLON

Cut the following

- [ ] 20 squares cut to the same size to match calico squares
- [ ] 1 large centre block to match large calico centre block
- [ ] 2 short and 2 long pieces to match calico sashing pieces.

Using a good steam iron with a power surge, press Pellon to the back of the matching calico pieces.

VLIESOFIX

- [ ] Trace out ribbon swags for the centre medallion on to the back of the Vliesofix. Iron to the back of the apricot fabric. Cut out accurately and put aside.
- [ ] Cut strips of Vliesofix 2.5 cm (1 in) wide and 8 m (8½ yd) in combined length. Iron Vliesofix to the folded quilt binding, so that the Vliesofix aligns with the folded edge of the binding. DO NOT PEEL PAPER BACKING OFF. Leave to one side
- [ ] Iron Vliesofix to the back of all the ribbon pieces except the narrow threading ribbons; again do not peel paper backing off until ribbons are being used.

TWENTY BLOCKS

Following the layout for each block, iron on ribbons and doilies if they are beneath other design elements or standing alone. If doilies are to be placed over a ribbon do not iron on, but rather wait until ribbons have been appliqued down. Iron on ribbons and doilies in the correct sequence; that is from the bottom layer up. The piece that is at the bottom goes on first, then the next piece and so on. The top piece is ironed on last. It is a good idea to number blocks so that you can identify them.

Complete each block before going on to the next one so that you can see how you are progressing.

CENTRE BLOCK AND SASHING

The preparation for the centre block and sashing is treated separately, on pages 58 and 59.

BUILDING A BLOCK

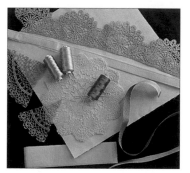

Assemble ribbons, doilies, laces and thread on the background fabric while you contemplate the design. If you are not sure or confident about how it looks, live with it for a while before cutting and fixing any of the elements to the fabric square. Iron fusible web (Vliesofix / Wonderunder) to the wrong side of embellishments.

Diagonal lines drawn in purple marking pen which fades over time are good guides for design placement. Note how the white doily was discarded. Press everything in place (working from the bottom layer, up to ensure the correct sequence for overlapping) then secure lace and doily segments with free motion embroidery using matching or monofilament thread and straight stitch.

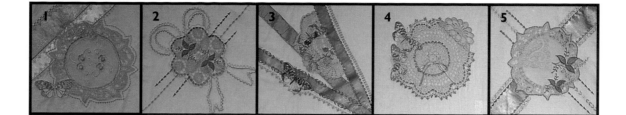

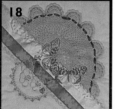

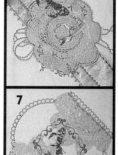

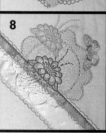

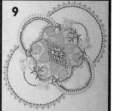

The Arsenic and Old Lace *quilt (pictured left) is composed of twenty small blocks which are numbered from 1 to 20 starting from the top left hand corner and progressing in a clockwise direction.*

After paying particular attention to preparation (I always find this the most boring part of the job but I still do it with patience and accuracy in order to save time in the long run) construct each block following the instructions beneath the photos on the following pages.

The centre block is the main feature and the whole design of small blocks and centre is banded by the sashing strips at sides, top and bottom.

Then the corners are rounded with scissors, the edge is piped with satin piping cord and bound with the double thickness binding strip. The finishing touch is the lace edging with its slightly gathered corners which is pinned to the stitch in the ditch line at the back of the quilt but attached by stitching in the ditch from the quilt front. You can see the lace edging clearly on page 75 where the quilt is pictured over the Dust Ruffle.

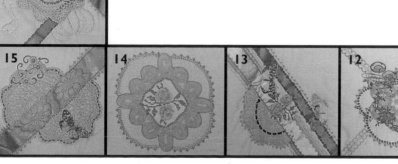

METHOD

ALL BLOCKS

1. Set machine up for free motion embroidery
   - use a disposable bobbin, tighten bobbin tension, lower feed dogs
   - thread Monofil in the needle with a tension between 2 and 3
   - 80 needle
   - darning/big foot for free motion stitching
   - straight stitch.

2. The movement of the fabric and the length of the stitch is now determined by the artist. Rule of thumb is to work with a fast machine and slow hands.

3. Think of the bed of your sewing machine as an ice rink, and the fabric as the skater. Slide the fabric in whichever direction you choose but keep it flat, never pull it up or it will catch on the needle and break the thread and needle. Practise and you will soon perfect this technique.

4. Use free motion embroidery to attach all doilies because the 'ins' and 'outs' of a doily's edge can be negotiated easily with this method of stitching. Attach doilies that are under ribbons first, stitching as close as possible to doily edges. I also like to catch them down around the centre of the design. This stabilising procedure is important so that the embroidery foot does not become snagged in the doily's lacy holes during the embroidering of the motifs.

5. When the doily placement is over a ribbon, applique ribbon down first before attaching doily.

BOW DESIGN
Use this same size in *Arsenic and Old Lace* quilt. Change tails and loops to suit your design.

BLOCK I

1. Cut one strip of 5 cm (2 in) wide coffee satin ribbon 20 cm (8 in) long.

2. Cut one strip of 3.5 cm (1½ in) wide apricot satin ribbon 30 cm (12 in) long.

3. Iron across top left hand corner of block so that they butt up to each other.

4. Applique top side of coffee ribbon down with 1055 thread and st. # 1.

5. Applique both sides of apricot ribbon down with 1053 st. # 5.

6. On the inside of all three rows of stitching, 1060 thread use st. # 14.

7. Iron 18 cm (7 in) Battenburg doily in the centre of the block to overlap apricot ribbon only. Stitch in place as with all doilies.

8. Using st. # 4 and 1060 thread outline the doily shape 1 cm (⅜ in) beyond its edge. On the inner edge use st. # 2 and thread 1055.

9. Using the above four coloured threads, embroider a floral motif in the centre of the doily, with a butterfly on each side.

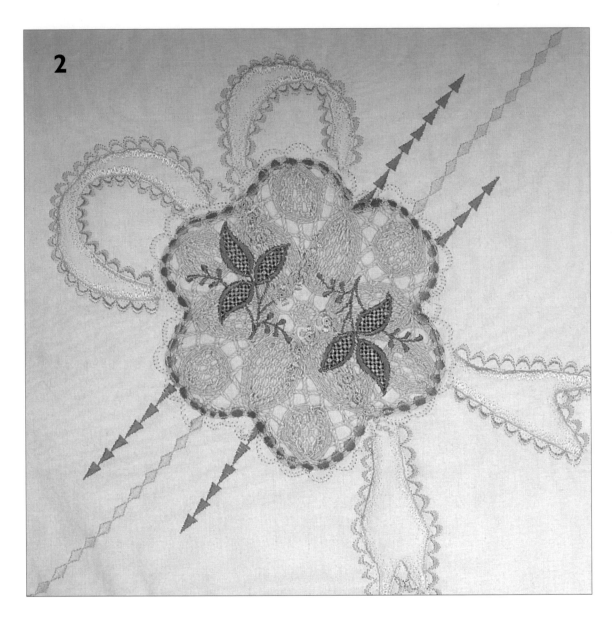

BLOCK 2

1. Draw in bow loops and tails as in photo-graph (see diagram on page 58) on either side of 13 cm (5 in) diameter doily.

2. Draw a diagonal line from the top right corner to the bottom left corner. Centre the doily on this diagonal line, pinning in place.

3. Extend parallel lines on either side of the doily and this centre line 2.5 cm (1 in) apart making the lines uneven in length around 4 cm – 7.5 cm (1⅝ in – 3 in).

4. Outline doily with st. #15 and thread colour 1053.

5. Embroider bow loops and tails with 1082 thread and st. # 6.

6. Outside edge of bow loops and tails embroider with 1060 thread and st. # 20.

7. Diagonal corner to corner line stitched 1053 thread and st. # 7.

8. Diagonal lines on either side of the above line stitched in 1306 thread and st. # 8.

9. Applique doily down with 1060 thread and st # 4 following doily shape.

10. Embroider two motifs in the centre of the doily using the above thread combinations.

BLOCK 3

1. Cut 3.5 cm (1½ in) wide coffee taffeta ribbon 43 cm (17 in) long and iron in place.

2. Applique with 1055 thread and st. # 12.

3. Measure 14 cm (5½ in) on either side of the top left hand corner and mark with a cross.

4. Cut green satin 2.5 cm (1 in) ribbon in two 33 cm (13 in) lengths. Pin in place between crosses and bottom right hand corner.

5. Cut 18 cm (7 in) doily in half, place cut edge of one piece under upper green ribbon with other edge overlapping coffee ribbon.

6. Applique lower green ribbon with thread 1306 and st. # 9. Use same thread and st. # 4 to applique edges of upper ribbon.

7. With thread 1053 and st. # 4, stitch a half circle to emphasise the inner design of doily and then do its edge the same.

8. Using the above thread colours plus 1055, embroider a flower motif and two butterflies.

9. Outline the lower edge profile of the lower green ribbon and butterfly with thread colour 1060 and st. # 14.

10. On the outside edge of upper green ribbon use thread 1060 and st. # 16.

BLOCK 4

1. Doily ironed in centre of block and stitched down.
2. Using thread 1306 and st. # 4 applique doily down just inside its outside edge.
3. Using thread 1126 and st. # 14 stitch around the outside edge of the doily shape.
4. Using thread 1060 and st. # 4 applique around the centre circle of the doily.
5. Using apricot fabric with Vliesofix ironed to the back, applique/embroider a lily design (see page 25) as per block design, using thread colour 1053.

6. Using the above thread combinations embroider two butterflies on the block to overlap doily.
7. Thread narrow apricot ribbon through small centre circle of the doily and tie ends in a small bow.

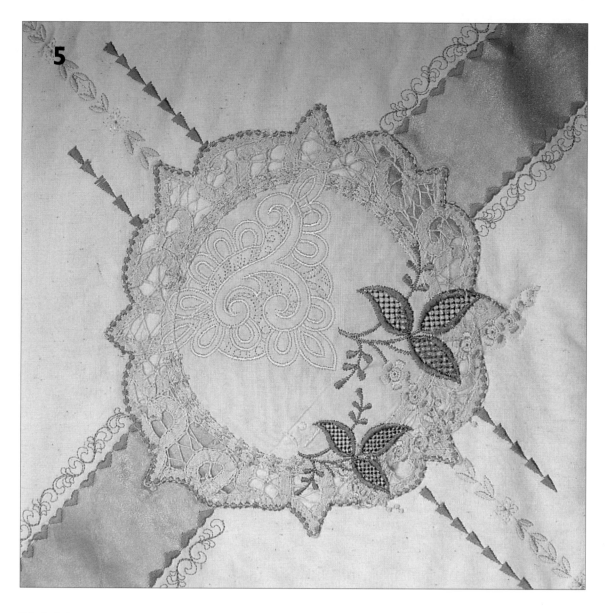

BLOCK 5

1. Cut a 43 cm (17 in) length of 5 cm (2 in) wide coffee satin ribbon and iron in place on diagonal from bottom left to top right corner.
2. Applique sides with thread 1055 st. # 3; beyond use st. # 17 in the same thread.
3. Rule line on the diagonal from top left corner to bottom right corner.
4. Iron 18 cm (7 in) diameter Battenburg doily in the centre of the block. Stitch down.
5. Draw in parallel lines 2.5 cm (1 in) on either side of the ruled line making them 5 cm (2 in) and 7 cm (3 in).

6. Centre line behind the doily is embroidered with thread 1053 and st. # 9.
7. Embroider shorter lines on either side in thread 1306 and st. # 8.
8. Applique doily down following the doily shape with thread 1055 and st. # 4.
9. Embroider around the centre fabric of the doily using 1060 and st. # 29.
10. Using the above thread combinations embroider two flower motifs and one cut work motif as in photograph.

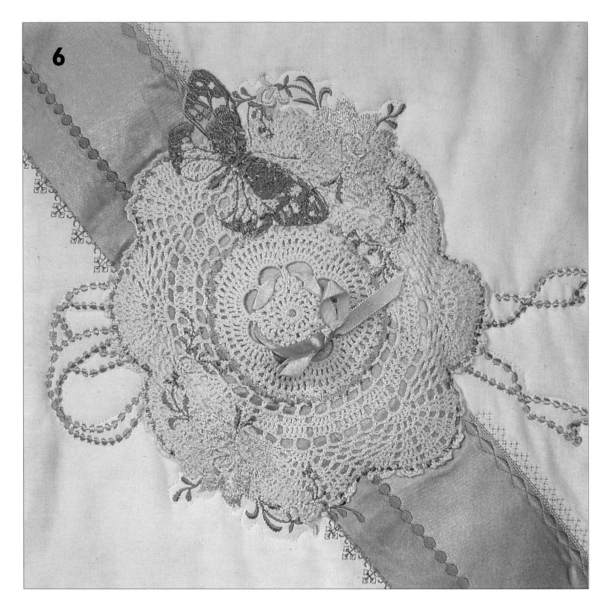

BLOCK 6

1. Cut 43 cm (17 in) length of 5 çm (2 in) wide coffee satin ribbon and iron in place on diagonal from top left to bottom right corner.

2. Cut 35 cm (14 in) length of 3 cm (1⅛ in) wide green satin ribbon, iron in place to the left of the coffee ribbon, butting up.

3. Applique bottom edge of green ribbon with thread 1306 st. # 14. Use the same thread and st. # 4 for the edge with coffee ribbon.

4. Applique outside edge of coffee ribbon thread 1053 and st. # 18. Inside on coffee ribbon use thread 1055 and st. # 7.

5. Thread pale cream ribbon through the centre holes of 18 cm (7 in) doily and iron in centre of block to overlap both ribbons.

6. Draw in bow loops and tails. Embroider with thread 1055 and st. # 4.

7. Using the same stitch and thread 1306 applique doily down following doily shape.

8. Using the same stitch and thread 1142 follow circle in doily centre.

9. Using threads 1126, 1053 and 1306 embroider two flower designs and one butterfly as per block photograph.

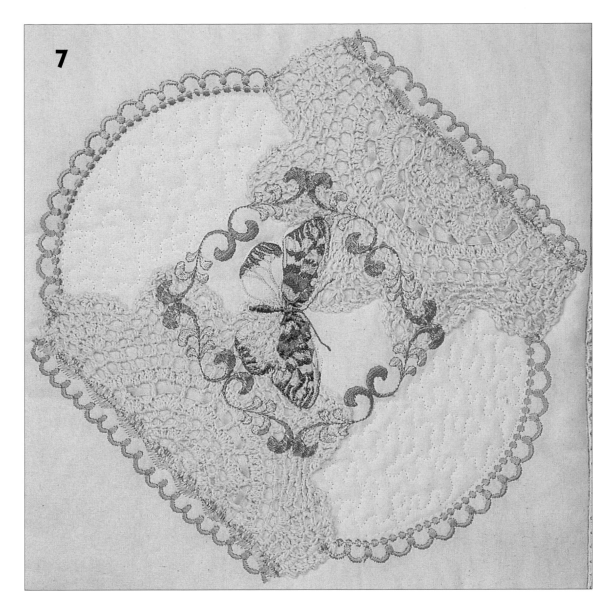

BLOCK 7

1. Thread narrow apricot ribbon through small circle in centre of 18 cm (7 in) diameter doily. Cut doily in half.
2. Iron in place so the straight sides are across opposite corners, and the half circles touch in the centre of the block.
3. Connect doily halves with arcs drawn around a saucer.
4. Stitch shaped sides of doily down with straight stitch.
5. Applique straight sides down with 1060 thread and st. # 2.

6. On the outside of this with the same thread st. # 21.
7. Again with the same thread stitch around the connecting arcs with st. # 4 and st. # 21 on the outside edge.
8. Using thread colours 1306, 1053 and 1126 stitch an open shield design with a butterfly (facing right) in the centre.

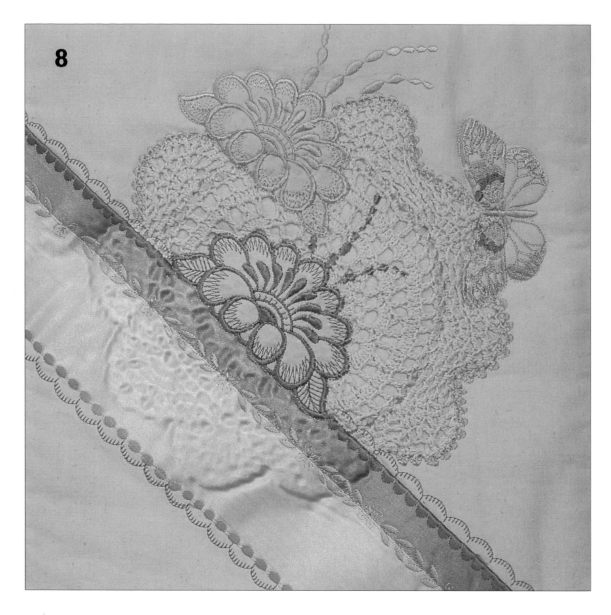

BLOCK 8

1. Iron 18 cm (7 in) doily in centre of block. Stitch down with matching thread.

2. Applique around the doily shape with thread 1060 and stitch # 23.

3. Follow the shape of the large inside circle stitching with thread 1053 and st. # 2.

4. Cut a 30 cm (12 in) length of 5 cm (2 in) wide apricot satin ribbon and iron across bottom left hand corner, covering doily edge.

5. Cut 38 cm (15 in) length of 2.5 cm (1 in) wide green satin ribbon and iron on the top side of apricot ribbon, covering more doily.

6. Using thread 1306 and st. # 13 applique outside edge of green ribbon in place.

7. Using thread 1053 and st. # 9 stitch down apricot ribbon where it meets green ribbon.

8. On the other edge of apricot ribbon with the above thread st. # 4; outside this row of stitching st. # 15 in thread 1306.

9. Using apricot fabric applique/embroider two lily motifs (see page 25), extending stamens with st. #2 use threads 1053 and 1306.

10. Again, using the above threads embroider a butterfly as per block photograph.

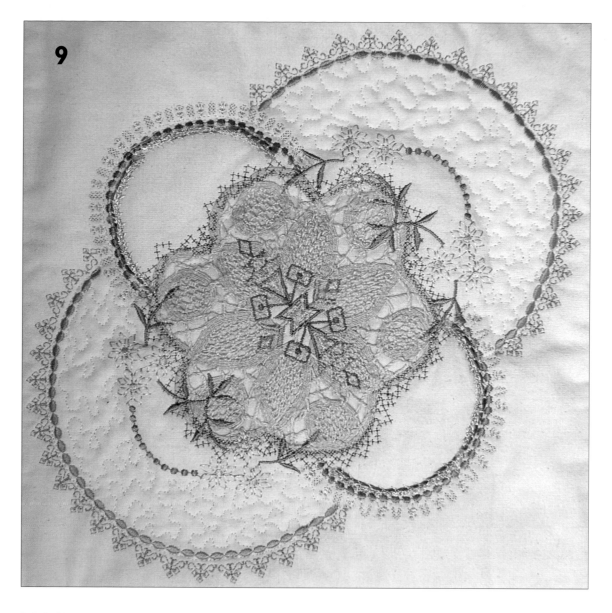

BLOCK 9

1. Iron small doily 13 cm (5 in) diameter in centre of block.

2. With blue marking pen and saucer and a glass as templates, extend design as per block photograph with two large half circles on top right to bottom left diagonal corners, and two small half circles on the opposite diagonals.

3. Using couching foot, and suitable matching couching threads, stitch down with thread 1053 and st. # 25 following small half circles.

4. Beyond this use thread 1306 and st. # 4, and beyond this again use thread 1053 and st. # 16.

5. With thread 1055 and st. # 2 follow curve of large half circle. Use the same thread and st. # 14 beyond the above.

6. Applique doily down with thread 1306 and st. # 18.

7. Using the above threads and 1126 embroider a motif in the centre of the doily.

8. On either side of the doily embroider a design that best matches the one which appears in the photograph.

BLOCK 10

1. Draw lines from corner to corner on the diagonals that cross in the centre of the block.

2. With thread colour 1053 and st. # 17 stitch on these lines.

3. On the outside edges of this row of stitching use thread 1306 and st. # 14.

4. Angle the square Battenburg doily so it becomes a diamond on the block (refer to photograph) and iron it in place.

5. Applique down at the junction where the lace meets the plain fabric with thread 1060 and st. # 13 following curves of the junction.

6. Use thread 1142 and st. # 23 beyond the outside edge of the doily shape.

7. Inside the above stitching and on the doily's edge embroider with thread 1142 and st. # 13.

8. Using the above threads, embroider a motif in the fabric centre of the doily.

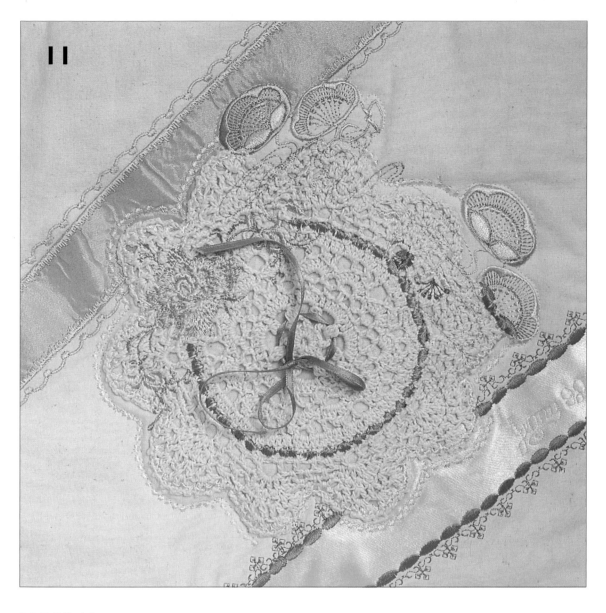

BLOCK 11

1. Cut a 28 cm (11 in) length of 3 cm (1⅛ in) wide coffee taffeta ribbon and iron across top left hand corner of block.

2. Cut a 22 cm (9 in) length of 5 cm (2 in) wide apricot satin ribbon and iron across diagonally opposite corner (see photo).

3. With thread 1060 and st. # 6 applique coffee ribbon on both sides. Outside these edges use same thread and st. # 21.

4. Use thread 1306 and st. # 2 to applique apricot ribbon on both sides. Same thread st. # 14 to embroider outside edge of stitching.

5. Thread narrow green ribbon through small circle in centre of 18 cm (7 in) doily and iron in centre of block to overlap both ribbons.

6. Stitch down with matching thread then applique with thread 1082 and st. # 12.

7. Beyond the outside edge, follow the doily shape using the same thread st. # 4.

8. Define larger of the two inner circles of doily with thread 1306 and st. # 2.

9. Using the above thread combinations embroider three flower motifs to straddle the doily and block as per photograph.

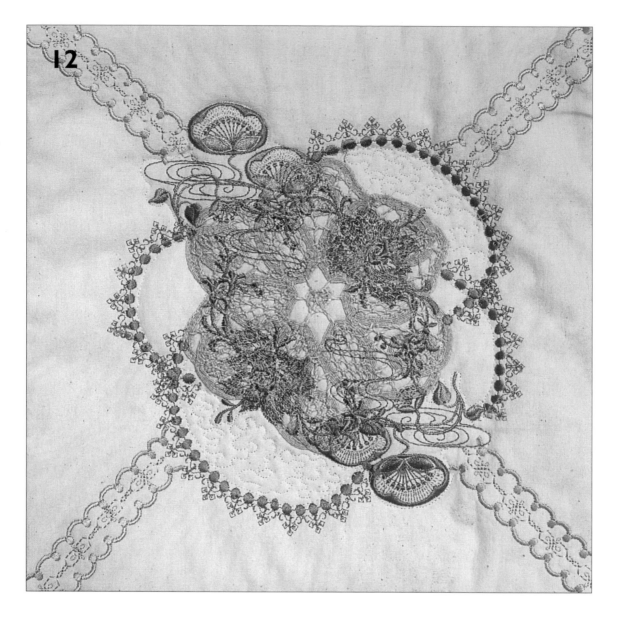

BLOCK 12

1. Draw lines diagonally across the block from corner to corner.

2. Iron 13 cm (5 in) diameter doily in centre of block.

3. Draw in two large and two small inter-locking half circles as per block photograph.

4. With thread 1060 and st. # 28 stitch on the diagonal lines up to the half circles on two sides, and up to the doily edge on the other two sides.

5. On the outside edges of these rows of stitching use the same thread and st. # 21.

6. Stitch interlocking half circle outlines with thread 1306 and st. # 4. Use same the thread and st. # 14 outside the outlines.

7. Use thread colours 1053, 1306 and 1142 to embroider two pairs of matching motifs on opposite sides of the doily as per block photograph.

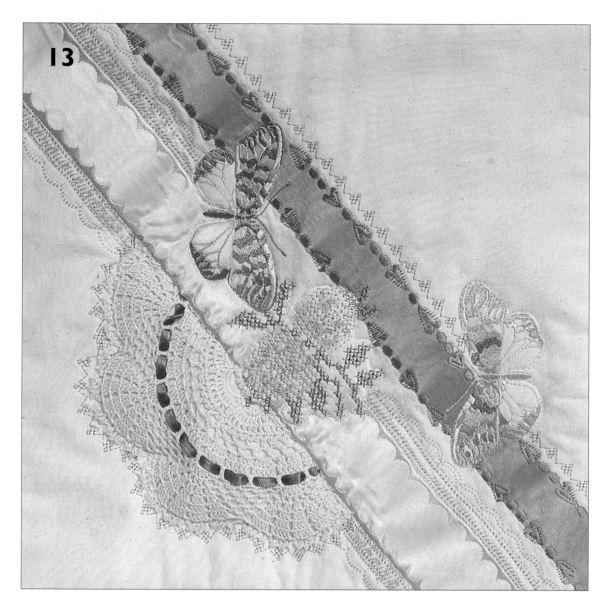

BLOCK 13

1. Cut 38 cm (15 in) length of 3 cm (1⅛ in) wide apricot satin ribbon. Mark the lower edge of the block 6 cm (2½ in) to left of right hand corner. Centre ribbon between top left corner and mark on the lower edge.

2. Thread narrow coffee ribbon through inner half circle of leftover half doily from block 3. Put straight side of doily under apricot ribbon, iron. Stitch down with matching thread.

3. Cut 38 cm (15 in) green satin ribbon, and iron in place 2.5 cm (1 in) up from apricot ribbon and parallel to it. Iron in place.

4. Applique apricot ribbon with 1053 and st. # 12 on both sides.

5. Outside the above stitching use thread 1084 and st. # 24. Outside this again use the same colour with st. # 15.

6. Applique green ribbon with 1306 and st. # 10; above top edge thread 1055, st. # 19.

7. Around outside edge of doily, do a row of stitching using the above thread and stitch.

8. Using the above thread combinations embroider one cross stitch motif and two butterflies as per block photograph.

BLOCK 14

1. Angle a 18 cm (7 in) square Battenburg doily so that it becomes a diamond shape in centre of the block and iron it in place. Stitch down with matching thread.

2. Connect its four corners by drawing around a plate.

3. Stitch over these lines with thread 1053 and st. # 4.

4. Outside the above row of stitching use thread 1306 and st. # 14.

5. Free motion stipple stitch inside each of the four arcs with thread 1084.

6. Applique doily down following the doily shape with the above thread and st. # 4. Using the same thread and st. # 12 stitch around the outside edge of the fabric centre of the doily.

7. Using the above threads embroider a cross stitch design in the centre of the doily.

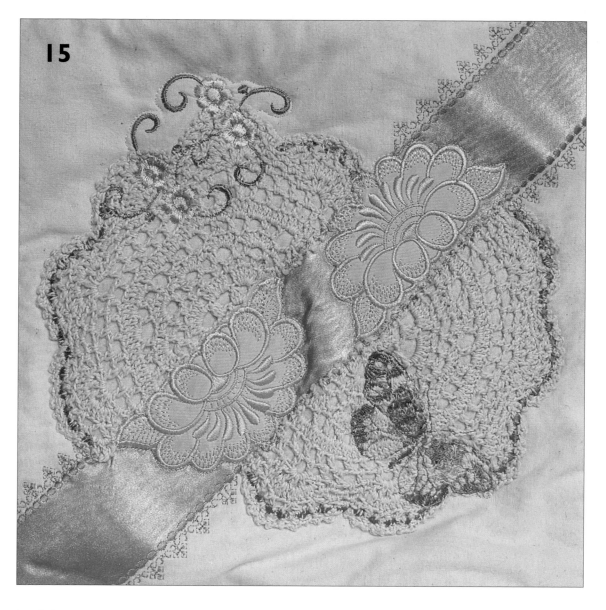

BLOCK 15

1. Cut an 18 cm (7 in) doily in half.

2. Cut a 43 cm (17 in) length of 5 cm (2 in) wide coffee coloured satin ribbon. Pin in place on the diagonal from bottom left corner to top right corner.

3. Slip straight edge of half doilies under the ribbon on opposite sides of the ribbon, just off centre to either side.

4. Stitch in place with matching thread.

5. Applique ribbon down on either side with thread 1055 and st. # 4.

6. Use the same thread and st. # 14 on the outside edge of the coffee coloured ribbon.

7. Using apricot fabric and matching thread 1053, either applique by hand or machine the two lily motifs (see page 25) along the ribbon as per block photograph.

8. Applique just inside the outside edge of doily halves with thread 1306 and st. # 4.

9. Using the above thread colours embroider one butterfly and one flower motif as per block photograph.

BLOCK 16

1. Cut a 33 cm (13 in) length of 2.5 cm (1 in) wide green satin ribbon. Measure 18 cm (7 in) from the bottom right corner in both directions and mark with cross. Iron ribbon in place between these two crosses.

2. Cut a 30 cm (12 in) length of 5 cm (2 in) wide coffee coloured satin ribbon and cross top right corner in the above manner.

3. Applique green ribbon in 1306, st. # 34.

4. Applique coffee ribbon in 1084, st. # 4.

5. Same thread and st. # 14 for outside edge of above row of stitching.

6. Iron 18 cm (7 in) doily in centre of block. Stitch down with matching thread.

7. Draw in bow loops and tails (see pages 32 and 58) and outline with 1082 and st. # 7. Free motion straight stitch with the same thread to give a shaded effect to ribbon.

8. Applique doily in place with 1053 and st. # 4. Highlight larger circle with same thread and st. # 2. Use same stitch and thread 1306 to embroider inner circle of doily.

9. Use above thread combinations to embroider three flower motifs.

BLOCK 17

1. Thread narrow coffee ribbon through outside circle of 18 cm (7 in) diameter doily before cutting doily in half.

2. Iron in place centred 4 cm (1½ in) from both sides of the block. Stitch down with matching thread.

3. Applique straight edges of doily with thread 1055 and st. # 13.

4. Applique curved doily edges with thread 1060 and st. # 4.

5. Draw two half circle ribbon loops (see pages 57 and 58 for patterns) to connect the two doily pieces top and bottom.

6. Use thread 1053 and st. # 4 to outline ribbon loops. Shade twists in the ribbon loops with same thread colour using straight stitch and free motion stitching.

7. Use thread 1306 and st. # 19 for the outside edges of ribbon loops.

8. Using the above thread colours, embroider a shield shape in the centre of the block with a butterfly motif in the centre of the shield.

BLOCK 18

1. Cut 41 cm (16 in) of 3 cm (1⅛ in) wide apricot satin ribbon and 33 cm (13 in) of 2.5 cm (1 in) wide green satin ribbon.

2. Cut a 25 cm (10 in) diameter lace doily in half and thread outer edge with coffee coloured narrow ribbon and inner curve with narrow apricot ribbon.

3. Place apricot ribbon on the top-left/bottom-right diagonal with top edge on diagonal line. Centre half doily on block with straight edge just under edge of ribbon. Iron on and stitch doily edge down with matching thread.

4. Iron green satin ribbon to bottom edge of apricot ribbon; applique with 1306, st. # 12 and apricot ribbon with 1053 and st. # 27

5. Using 1053 and st. # 22 embroider outside edge of green ribbon.

6. Draw a small half circle (use a glass) with its diameter on lower side of the green ribbon. Outline this figure with thread 1053 and st. # 4. Use thread 1306 and st. # 14 to work the outside edge of the half circle.

7. Using the above threads, work two butterfly motifs and one outline motif.

BLOCK 19

1. Iron 13 cm (5 in) diameter doily in centre of block. Stitch down with matching thread.

2. Draw in three interlocking half circles (loops) to the left of the block using a cup as a template for the small one on the left and a saucer for the other two.

3. Draw in ribbon tails (see pages 58 and 59) to the right of the block as in photograph.

4. With thread 1142 and st. # 4, outline ribbons and interlocking loops.

5. With thread 1306 and st. # 14 stitch around the outside of the above.

6. Using the above threads plus 1126 embroider two lily motifs (see page 25) and one butterfly as in block photograph.

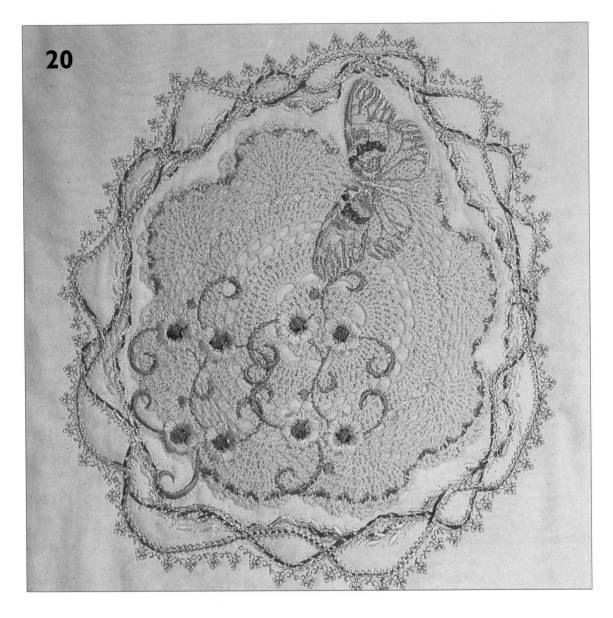

20

BLOCK 20

1. Iron 18 cm (7 in) doily in centre of block and stitch down with matching thread.

2. Use thread 1306 and st. # 3 to applique down the edge of the doily.

3. Use thread 1053 and st. # 3 to highlight the inner circle on the doily.

4. Using the above threads and 1126 embroider two flower motifs and one butterfly as in block photograph.

5. Place apricot, coffee and gold couching threads through couching foot. Select thread 1082 and st. # 26, 25 and 27 and couch down threads in three meandering circles around the doily.

6. Use thread 1055 and st. # 14 to work around the outside edge of the final meandering row of couching.

7. This is the last of the twenty blocks. Trim off any excess threads and backing stabilizer, remove any blue pen lines with a damp cloth and press blocks flat. Square up blocks using the method described in Joining Quilted Blocks in Tips, Tricks and Techniques on page 15 and place aside ready to join up.

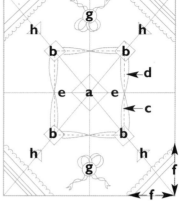

CENTRE BLOCK PLACEMENT DIAGRAM

LAYOUT KEY

a. Square centre doily is angled to a diamond shape.

b. Four square doilies are also angled as diamonds 30 cm (12 in) from centre doily along the four diagonal lines.

c. Broken lines indicate swag placement.

d. Swags are the connecting elements between the four doily diamonds.

e. On both sides of the central doily there are two 20 cm (8 in) strips of tatted edging lace 2 cm (¾ in) apart.

f. Measure 38 cm (15 in) from corner to determine coffee satin ribbon/lace placement.

g. Placement for circular doilies over machine embroidered bows and loops.

h. Richelieu cut work embroidery motif placement is 51 cm (20 in) along diagonal lines from the centrally placed diamond doily.

CENTRE BLOCK

Finished size 81 cm x 135 cm (32 in x 53 in). The centre block is a feature of the quilt and calls for symmetrical designs and accurate placement. Work from the bottom 'layer' up when assembling the design elements. Again, this is another wonderful learning curve.

NOTE

When working with quilting and machine embroidery, remember that the fabric can shrink and the shape can become distorted. When working out placement positions, always measure from the centre out. This keeps the design square because the centre point remains fixed.

PREPARATION

☐ Cut calico block 83 cm × 137 cm (32½ in × 54 in) and fuse Pellon to the back.

☐ With a blue pen draw lines between the mid points of top and bottom and the sides of the rectangle. Also draw diagonal lines between opposite corners through the centre.

PLACEMENT POSITIONS

☐ Referring to the placement diagram (previous page) mark the following positions. Pin appropriate fabric pieces in place as you go. When satisfied, iron them in place.

☐ Centre square doily (a), angled to become a diamond.

☐ Measure 30 cm (12 in) from the centre on all four diagonal lines to position the centre of each of the four square doilies (b) which are also angled to become diamonds.

☐ Connecting lines on the square between the above four doilies are guides for applique ribbon swags (c).

☐ Enlarge and trace out centre block swags onto apricot fabric from pattern provided (see page 57), cut out and pin in place just under the doily edge.

LACE, RIBBON AND BRAID

☐ Cut 2.5 cm (¾ in) wide tatted edging lace into four equal lengths each 20 cm (8 in). Place two parallel strips, straight sides facing, 2 cm (¾ in) apart between either side of centre doily and the enclosing swag (e). Again, lace just sits under doily and swag on each end.

☐ Measure and mark points 33 cm (12 in) from each corner and connect with straight lines across each corner (f). These are the lines for lace and ribbon placement across each corner.

☐ Cut four strips of 7.5 cm (3 in) wide edging lace 46 cm (18 in) long. Pin across each corner on the ruled line, scalloped edge on line.

☐ Cut two strips of 5 cm (2 in) wide coffee satin ribbon 33 cm (13 in) long and pin along straight edge of lace on top left and bottom right corners.

☐ Cut two strips of 5 cm (2 in) wide apricot satin ribbon 33 cm (13 in) long and pin along straight edge of lace on top right and bottom left corners.

☐ Cut two strips of 1 cm (¾ in) wide cream flat braid 33 cm (13 in) long and another two strips 27 cm (10½ in) long, and pin in place on apricot satin ribbon with the shorter pieces closest to the corners.

☐ Cut two strips of 2 cm (1¼ in) wide straight sided lace 22 cm (8½ in) long and pin in place leaving a 2 cm (¾ in) gap between this lace and apricot ribbon.

DOILIES, BOWS AND MOTIFS

☐ Measure 30 cm (12 in) above and below the centre point on the vertical line and pin the two remaining Battenburg doilies in place (g).

☐ Using a blue pen, draw in bow loops and tails (see page 32) at top and bottom of each of the above doilies.

☐ From the centre on the diagonal lines, measure 51 cm (20 in) in both directions to determine the placement position for Richelieu cut work embroidery motif (h).

☐ Making sure all fabric pieces are accurately positioned, iron in place so that they are flat and even, removing pins as you go.

Below: Side sashing piece showing embroidered motifs.

METHOD

CENRE BLOCK

1. As with previous work stitch all lace and doilies down with matching thread.

2. With thread 1060 and st. # 17 embroider along the centre space between the tatted lace on either side of centre doily.

3. Using threads 1060 and 1082 embroider a cut work motif in centre of doily.

4. Applique doily around the centre fabric in thread 1306 and st. # 4.

5. Applique doily around edges with the above thread and st. # 2 then do the outside edge with st. # 14.

6. Applique ribbon swags with small satin stitch in thread colour 1053. For the outside edge of ribbon swags have the same thread and st. # 14.

7. Shading on the swags is achieved firstly by free motion stitching in thread 1082, then thread 1053.

8. Inside the applique, stitch in thread 1082 and st. # 13. Work all swags the same.

9. Work all four corner doilies the same with the inside square in thread 1053 and st. # 4 and the outside lace edge appliqued in thread 1055 and st. # 23.

10. Using only the thread colours from the thread list, embroider motifs as shown in the photograph on page 53, matching colours, positions and designs.

11. Treat top and bottom doilies the same. Stitch circular Battenburg doilies around their edges with matching thread.

12. Using thread 1082 st. # 6 embroider bow loops and tails. Embroider outside edges of the above rows with thread 1060 st. # 14.

13. Embroider two flower motifs in centres of both doilies.

14. Using thread 1084 embroider cut work designs on the diagonals (h).

15. Stitch lace down with matching thread in all four corners.

16. Coffee ribbon is appliqued on both sides with thread 1126 st. # 2. On the edge closest to the corner use the same thread st. # 14.

17. Select thread 1084 st. # 23 to applique scalloped lace edge on the two lace pieces in the apricot ribbon corners.

18. Applique apricot ribbon with same thread st. # 2 on both sides of ribbon. Stitch braid down on the inside edge of these stitches. Centre is now complete.

SASHING PIECES

1. Enlarge and trace bow and tail designs from pattern (see page 57) and centre on all four sashing pieces.

2. Embroider all bows and tails with thread 1082 st. # 6. For the outside edges use thread 1306 st. # 14. Iron circular medallions in place in centre of each bow and applique with the same thread and st. # 13.

3. Embroider seven butterflies (or applique or apply lace) as in photo (see below) on both long sashing pieces; short pieces are plain.

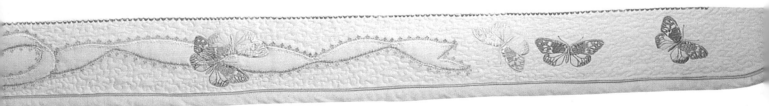

ASSEMBLING THE QUILT

PRESSING AND JOINING

1. Press and square up all blocks carefully as per instructions in the front of the book (see page 15).
2. Join blocks into four strips – two for top and bottom and two for sides. Top blocks: 1 – 5, bottom blocks: 11 – 15. Left side blocks: 16 – 20. Right side blocks: 6 – 10. Put aside.
3. There are two different methods of putting the quilt together and quilting it.

METHOD 1: ALL IN ONE PIECE

1. Join quilt in one piece – centre with blocks around it and sashing pieces on the sides. Cut out backing fabric to fit remembering to leave 5 cm (2 in) on all sides extra.
2. Using the bonding technique described on page 13, attach the quilt backing to the pieced quilt.
3. Using 50 denier cream Tanne thread in bobbin and needle, starting from the centre out, outline quilt all doilies, ribbons, swags and lace pieces. Stitch in the ditch between each block, centre medallion and sashing.
4. Free motion stipple quilt the centre medallion outside ribbon swag area as in photograph.
5. Free motion quilt in selected blocks as per block photographs.
6. Using a smaller stipple quilting stitch, quilt all four sashing strips.
7. Use apricot thread 1053 and st. # 13 (with the scallops facing into the centre) around the outside edge of the centre medallion.
8. Repeat on the outside edge of the joined blocks so that the scallop faces away from the centre.
9. Press quilt and trim around the edges, rounding the corners.

10. Measure 2.5 cm (1 in) from quilt edge and attach satin piping all around the quilt.
11. Take prepared binding strip and attach binding strip in the same stitch line as the piping, following the method on page 000.
12. Fold binding over and press in place, easing in each corner. Stitch in the ditch to attach the back binding. (If you have a good steam iron this step is not really necessary because the Vliesofix alone will hold the binding.)

METHOD 2: QUILT AS YOU GO

1. Cut backing fabric 2.5 cm (1 in) wider on all sides for centre block. Attach with bond powder and quilt as for method 1.
2. Then cut backing fabric again 2.5 cm (1 in) wider on all sides for the four block strips – top, bottom and two sides.
3. Join one block strip to the centre with right sides together, then attach backing fabric for the block strip in the same seam, again with right sides together. Attach block strip backing fabric with the bonding technique explained on page 13, and quilt as for Method 1.
4. Repeat on three other sides.
5. Repeat for sashing pieces, until quilt is complete, then finish off with piping and binding repeating steps 10, 11 and 12 in the first method.

ATTACHING THE EDGING LACE

Attach edging lace by pinning from the back in the stitch-in-the-ditch line of stitching. Gather lace at the corners slightly so it sits flat. Attach from front of quilt by stitching in the ditch. Your quilt is now complete and its love and artistry will be enjoyed by you and your family now and generations to come.

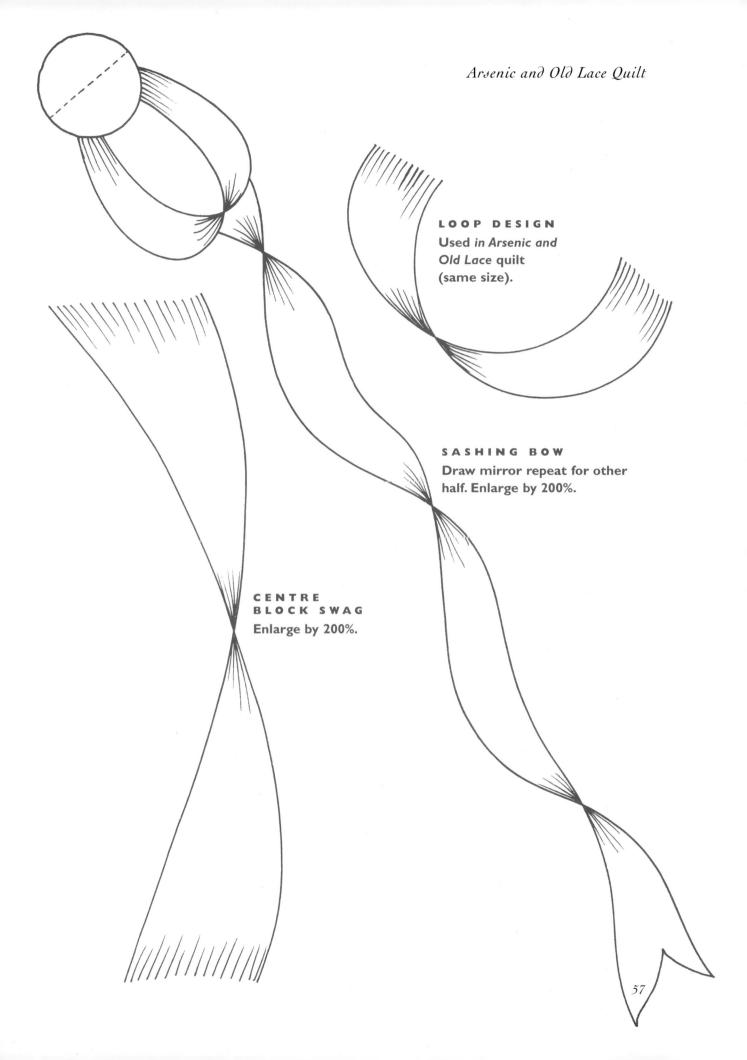

LOOP DESIGN
Used *in Arsenic and
Old Lace* quilt
(same size).

SASHING BOW
Draw mirror repeat for other
half. Enlarge by 200%.

**CENTRE
BLOCK SWAG**
Enlarge by 200%.

BOW DESIGN
Used in *Arsenic and Old Lace*
quilt (same size).

LOOP DESIGN
Used in *Arsenic and Old Lace*
quilt (same size).

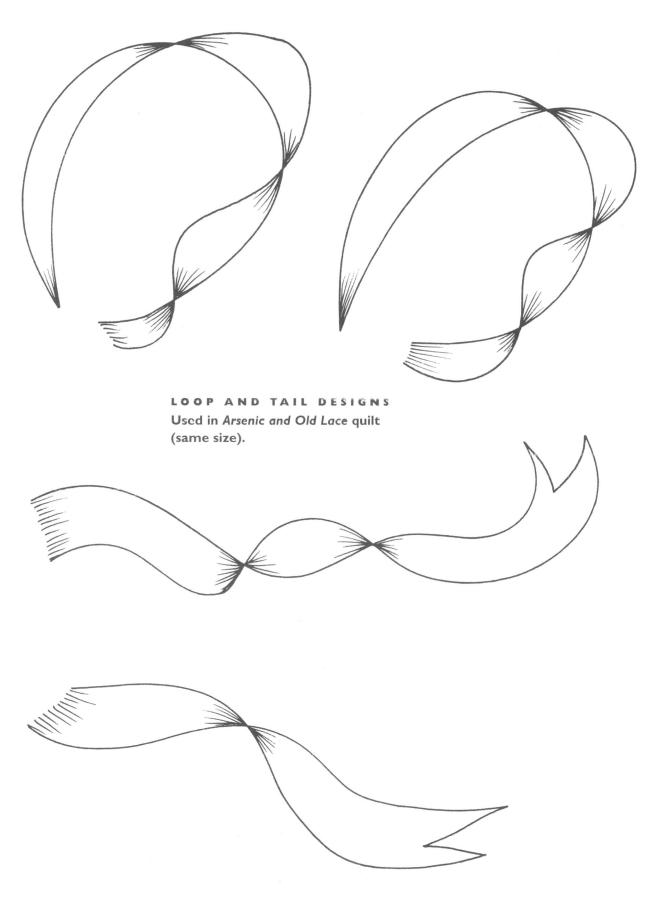

LOOP AND TAIL DESIGNS
Used in *Arsenic and Old Lace* quilt
(same size).

MATERIALS

- Lampshade with top diameter 13 cm (5 in), bottom diameter 38 cm (15 in), height 25 cm (10 in)
- .5 m (½ yd) of 150 cm wide unbleached calico (muslin)
- 1.3 m (1½ yd) of 10 cm (4 in) wide edging lace to match quilt, tea dyed if necessary
- 1 m (39 in) narrow elastic for top and bottom casing of cover
- 80/90 large eyed needle
- 1 reel of cream Madeira Tanne 50 construction thread and matching bobbin
- Madeira pre-wound bobbin
- Madeira Rayon 40 in colours 1053, 1054, 1084, 1060, 1306 and 1071 (off white)
- Pins, scissors, quilting ruler, tape measure, photocopy paper, blue fabric marking pen, Crisp spray starch

Lampshade

Mood lighting invites and soothes. Soft lighting diffused through a cream lampshade gives a flattering finish to any room. Following my instructions, this ever-so-easy lampshade can be made in no time. The cutting method produces a cover that is softly gathered at the top.

PREPARATION

- Cut out calico 132 cm × 45 cm (52 in × 17¾ in). Fold in half on the short side and press flat.
- From the top on both short sides, measure down 33 cm (13 in) and mark with fabric marking pen. On the upper edge, measure in 15 cm (6 in) from the raw edges on one side and the folded edge on the other side and mark.
- Draw lines from first marks to second marks (cutting diagram). Sloped sides correspond with lampshade, and lessen the fabric bulk at the top. Extend both sloped lines AC and BD to point E which is way above the fabric. Mark the distance between E and C on a tape measure or ruler and keeping E as a fixed point and the fabric steady, scribe an arc to D, marking as you go with marking pen. Then scribe another arc with radius measuring the distance between A and E. Cut allowing for a 1 cm (¼ in) seam allowance around the bottom.

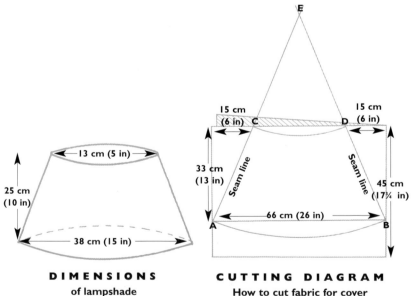

DIMENSIONS
of lampshade

CUTTING DIAGRAM
How to cut fabric for cover

M E T H O D

For variety and interest, use the same group of coloured threads for each floral motif but vary their order when embroidering each of the four roses on the lampshade.

THE COVER

1. Using cream thread stitch up side seams with a large stitch. Test that the fabric sits flat and tight over the lampshade without gathers at the bottom edge. When satisfied, stitch side seams with normal straight stitch. Press seams open from the wrong side, topstitch on either side of the seam line from the right side of the fabric.

2. Fold under a small hem on both top and bottom and stitch down. Turn under 1 cm (¼ in) casing for elastic at top and bottom and stitch down.

3. Measure up from the bottom hem approximately 5 cm (2 in) and draw a line parallel to the bottom curve of the fabric.

4. Attach lace along this line, from the right side, with a small zigzag stitch.

5. Place paper behind as a stabilizer and using apricot thread and st. # 13 cover stitching where lace is attached to fabric. Remove paper backing. Change to dark apricot thread and st. # 18 and stitch against the straight side of the previous row of scallops, onto the calico.

6. Matching the seams, wrong sides together (which already mark the mid points) divide lampshade cover into four equal parts by pressing both outer folded edges with an iron. With marking pen, draw lines on the two new divisions.

7. On all these four lines which divide the cover into quarters mark up 6 cm (2½ in) from where the lace meets the calico. These are the centres of the flower motifs.

8. Find the middle again between these four lines, press and mark. Now the lampshade is divided into eighths. On the four new lines, come up from the lace edge 7.5 cm (3 in) and mark with pen. These marks are the centres of the swags which are topped with the cream curlicue motifs. Come up again 3 cm (1¼ in) on these same four lines and mark with a cross for centres of the bows.

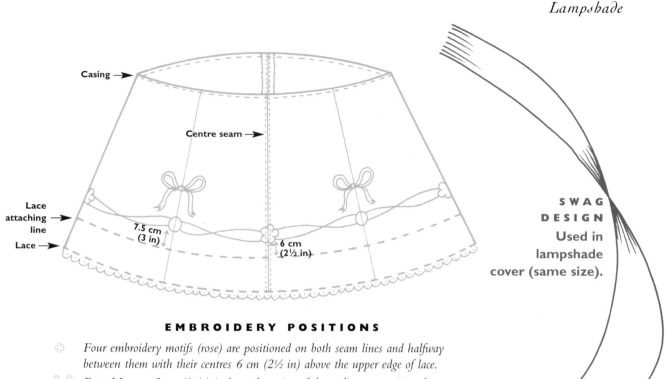

Casing →

Centre seam →

Lace attaching line →

Lace →

7.5 cm (3 in)

6 cm (2½ in)

SWAG DESIGN
Used in lampshade cover (same size).

EMBROIDERY POSITIONS

✿ *Four embroidery motifs (rose) are positioned on both seam lines and halfway between them with their centres 6 cm (2½ in) above the upper edge of lace.*

🎀 *Bow. Measure 3 cm (1¼ in) above the point of the curlicue to position the centre of embroidered bow.*

○ *Marks the centres of swags, 7.5 cm (3 in) from upper edge of lace, over which embroidered curlicues (four in all) are centred.*

⋈ *Twist in swag.*

THE EMBROIDERY

1. Using a blue marking pen, draw in the twisted ribbon swags.

2. Using paper as a backing stabilizer, apricot thread and st # 6 embroider over the swag lines, tapering stitch as the swag twists. Work on both inner edges of the swags, with the straight

Between the roses, the swag is topped with a curlicue with an embroidered bow above.

edge of the stitch following the swag lines.

3. Embroider the outside of these stitches, using dark apricot thread and st. # 4 reduced to its smallest size. Remove paper from back.

4. Position a flower motif where marked on each of the first four divisions, a bow on each of the second four divisions with a small curlicue design above.

5. Trim off excess threads from front and back, remove blue lines with damp cloth and press with Crisp spray starch.

6. Thread elastic through top and bottom casing, remember to leave enough slack so that the shade cover will stretch over the bottom circle. The top circle of course is pulled in tightly.

7. When satisfied that the gathers are correct do not sew ends together. Fasten them instead with small safety pins to enable the elastic to be easily removed for washing and ironing the lampshade cover.

Tablecloth

For the table you can make
your cloth from scratch, embellish
a cloth from your linen cupboard or
purchase a new one as I did. It was
white linen with a wide lace edge and
some drawn thread work so I dyed it
with my tea dye mixture to a soft
coffee/cream to blend with the quilt.
With both the tablecloth and lampshade, you can make them as ornate or
as plain as you like; there are no rules, so
please yourself. Just to show that these
Arsenic and Old Lace projects are versatile, I have shown the tablecloth here in
a romantic outdoor setting.

NOTE

If you are making your own tablecloth, you will need to do your hemstitching with the wing needle then the embroidery before you attach the lace edging. Remember that hem stitches go back and forth in the same hole several
times so it is important not to retard or pull the fabric. The state-of-the-art
machines today feed fabric through evenly ensuring perfect stitching at all
times. Just keep your fabric straight and let your machine do the rest.

MATERIALS

- One purchased tablecloth measuring 112 cm (48 in) square including lace edging OR fabric and lace to make the above
- One square of linen fabric 87 cm (34½ in) square
- 5.10 m (5½ yd) lace edging 18 cm (7 in) wide
- Circular doily 21 cm (8½ in) diameter
- Madeira Rayon 40 thread in colours 1053, 1054, 1082, 1060, 1306 and 1055
- Pre-wound bobbins by Madeira for embroidery
- Construction thread: Madeira Tanne 50 cream and matching bobbin
- 80/90 machine needle
- Open toed foot
- 120 wing needle (if you are making your own cloth)
- Pins, scissors, Crisp spray starch, large quilting ruler, tape measure, water fading pen, photocopy paper

PREPARATION

TO MAKE TABLECLOTH

- Cut out linen square. Iron several times misting with spray starch before each time; the build-up of starch acts as a stabilizer and adds body to the fabric.
- Turn up a 1 cm (¼ in) hem on all sides. Turn up again 3.5 cm (1½ in) to make an-other hem (this will be the wrong side). Mitre corners on the wrong side, seam the mitre, trim to 1 cm (¼ in) seam allowance and press flat. Pin hem in place, making sure corners are flat and accurate.
- From right side, using cream 50 thread and 120 wing needle attach hem with a suitable hem stitch.
- Measure up from this row of hemstitch 11.5 cm (4½ in). Using your quilting ruler draw a square with sides parallel to the first row of hemstitching. Using

another hemstitch and a 120 wing needle stitch over these lines.

PLACEMENT LINES

- Using your quilting ruler again, divide the square in half, both vertically and horizontally through the centre point. Then do the same on the diagonal.
- Measure out from the centre on all eight lines 16.5 cm (6½ in), mark with crosses to give placement positions for embroidered motifs which will form a circle.
- Measure 6 cm (2½ in) out from the corner of the second row of hemstitching on the four diagonal lines and mark with crosses. These will be the centres of the corner heart motifs.

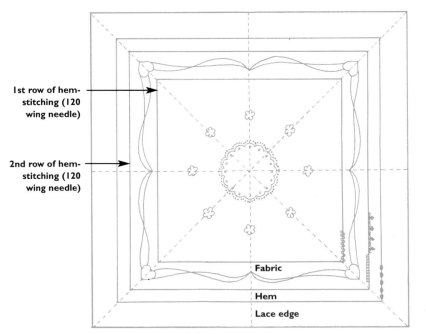

1st row of hem-stitching (120 wing needle)

2nd row of hem-stitching (120 wing needle)

Fabric

Hem

Lace edge

EMBROIDERY PLACEMENT

KEY FOR DIAGRAM

♡ *Hearts and bows embroidery placement*

✿ *Flower embroidery placement*

..... *Embroidery stitch*

⌐ *Mitred corner (from wrong side)*

⤬ *Swag lines for embroidery*

∿∿∿ *Lace embroidery*

METHOD

1. Using apricot thread and st. # 14 stitch around the outer edge of the first row of hem stitching on all four sides.

2. Pin doily in centre of fabric square. Attach with small zigzag stitch and matching thread, following the doily shape. Carefully cut fabric away from underside of doily.

3. Using paper as stabilizer, apricot thread and st. # 4 outline the doily. Remove paper stabilizer.

4. Using the eight previously marked crosses, embroider a flower on each one using only the threads listed in the materials.

5. Embroider a heart and bow design in each corner centring on the marked cross. This design is a personal one of mine, beautifully digitized by Angie Spong. While fabric is still in the hoop, select several small flower designs and embroider these also to add to the overall effect.

6. Link hearts with swags drawn with blue pen. If you have trouble drawing these in free hand, use the same size pattern at right or a blue flexible curve and trace around it. Embroider the inside edges of the swags with apricot thread and st. # 13 then decorate the outside edge with st. # 15 and dark apricot thread.

7. Butt lace flat against the hemmed edge of tablecloth. Using cream thread and small zigzag, stitch lace to the edge of the linen square, mitring corners as you go.

8. Place paper behind the lace as stabilizer. Select st. # 4 and apricot thread to embroider the linen whilst catching the edge of the lace at the same time on all four sides.

9. Remove all fabric pen lines, excess threads and stabilizer. Iron with Crisp spray starch to give that just out of grandmother's trunk look and smell.

SWAG DESIGN
For tablecloth (same size).

Adding small flowers to the heart and bow motif in the corner.

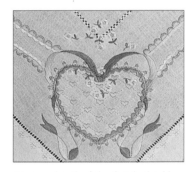

Corner detail of the finished tablecloth showing small flowers.

Swag is mirror reversed on the other side of the heart motif.

Rose motifs are equally spaced around central doily. Note the positions of the stems.

MATERIALS

- Store bought pillow slip with a flanged edge/flat border (see note on page 70)
- Tatted doily, 12 cm (5 in) diameter
- 15 cm square of Vliesofix/ Wonderunder
- 3 m (3⅓ yd) of 10 cm (4 in) wide edging lace (tea/coffee dyed to match quilt)
- 50 cm (20 in) of 15 mm (½ in) wide cream satin ribbon
- Madeira Rayon 40 thread in colours 1084, 1338, 1017, 1142, 1054 and 1306 plus thread to match the pillow sham fabric
- 120 wing needle
- Pins, scissors, water fading pen, fabric stabilizer, 'Stick-it-all' for hoop, photo copy paper for stitching, ruler.

PREPARATION

- Dye pillow slip in tea/coffee solution to match quilt. Also dye edging lace a deeper shade to match the lace around the quilt.
- Using a water fading pen, draw in bow loops and tails (see page 71 for pattern) in bottom left hand corner of pillow slip.
- Iron Vliesofix/Wonderunder to the back of the doily. Cut doily in quarters and then divide and cut two of the quarters into eighths.

Pillow Sham

Doily segments, machine embroidery and edging lace decorate this delightful pillow sham which, as its name implies, is more decorative than practical and is designed to be removed from the bed at night. I started with an antique pillow slip with self–covered buttons at its back opening and added a selection of *Arsenic and Old Lace* embellishments. In order to have a matched pair I plan to make another with the design flipped over so it will be a mirror reverse of the original.

METHOD

1. Work bow loops and tails with thread 1084 and st. # 13 with the straight side of the stitch on the blue lines. On the outside edge of these stitches work st. # 14 in thread colour 1054. Remember to use photo copy paper beneath the fabric as a stabilizer and remove when stitching is complete.

2. Iron the three doily segments in place so they fan out from bow tail. Applique down with st. # 13 and thread colour 1084 with the scallops either facing towards the centre of each piece or away from it. You may also choose to stitch build with st. # 15 and thread colour 1017.

3. Select a rose from your embroidery motifs and embroider around bow loops and tails as in the photograph using thread colours from the materials list but changing the order in repeated designs for variety. Select one large rose for corner.

4. Select butterflies and embroider amongst the roses in thread colours 1084, 1017 and 1338.

Lace edged pillow sham is decorated with a segmented doily, embroidered butterflies, rose motifs and a generous embroidered bow.

::::::::::::: **NOTE** :::::::::::::

You can buy a new flanged pillow slip and tea/coffee dye it (see page 70) to go with the quilt or make one. In order to fit a 48 cm x 69 cm (18 in x 27 in) pillow, the pillow part is around 50 cm x 75 cm (20 in x 29½ in) with a 5 cm (2 in) flange extension on all sides. Make the back and front the same depth but cut the back around 25 cm (10 in) wider in order to accommodate an opening, overlap and seams. When starting from scratch, it is easier to embroider the bow, attach doily pieces and work the rose motifs on the front before joining the back sections (cut the back in two to make an opening) to the front. Then hem the edges of the opening and align the overlap of back sections before joining front and backs together (raw edges and rights sides together). Turn to right side and press. At this stage, hemstitch the 'channel' between the pillow and the flange. In order for this hemstitched strip to be somewhat translucent, the back of it is cut away carefully with scissors and only the single layer of the front remains.

5. Iron doily quarter in top right hand corner. Cut ribbon in half and thread pieces from outer edges of top to the centre point and tie excess in small bow. Applique the doily quarter down as with previous doily pieces.

6. If you want to make a hemstitched border, first iron the outer edge of pillow sham with several mistings of Crisp spray starch; the starch acts as a stabilizer.

7. On the front of the pillow sham, measure in 5 cm (2 in) from the outside edge on all four sides and with ruler and pen draw a rectangular guide line for the outer row of hemstitching. From this measure 1 cm (½ in) towards the centre of pillow sham and draw a second guide line inside the first. Select a suitable hem stitch and using the wing needle and thread to match the colour of your pillow sham fabric, stitch over these lines.

8. If you want the channel between the rows of hemstitching to be more translucent than the rest of the pillow sham, carefully trim away the back layer of fabric with sharp scissors.

9. Pin lace flat against the outer edge of the outer row of hem stitching, remembering to gather lace slightly at corners so it will sit flat.

10. Using thread colour 1017 and st. # 13, scallops facing out, stitch over and applique lace down on its straight edge. Repeat this stitch and thread colour on the other side of the inside row of the stitching, with the scallops facing the centre of the pillow sham.

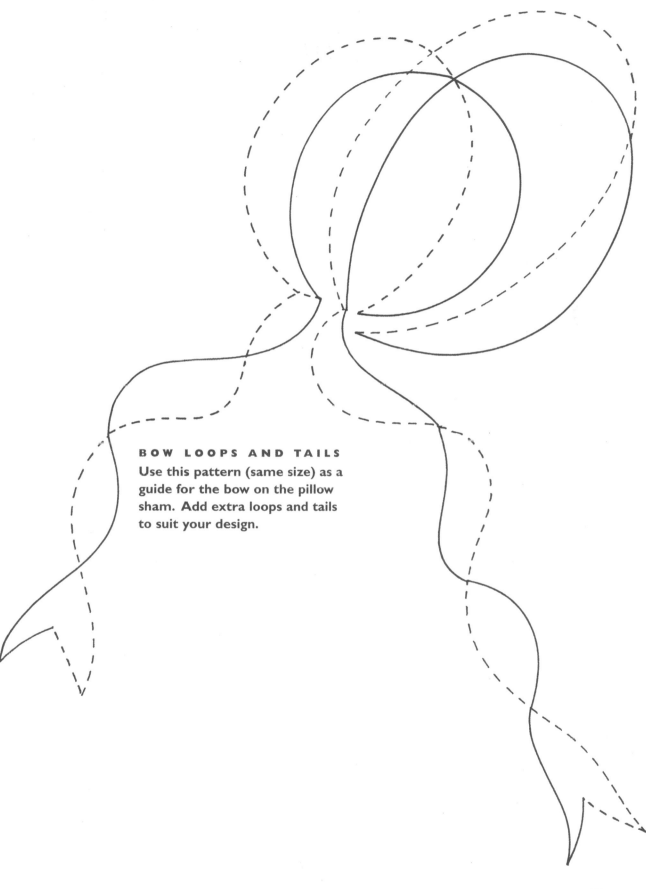

BOW LOOPS AND TAILS
Use this pattern (same size) as a
guide for the bow on the pillow
sham. Add extra loops and tails
to suit your design.

MATERIALS

- [ ] 13.5 m (15 yd) of 137 cm (54 in) wide cream netting for net, frill and circle at top. Take width of your net into consideration when calculating the amount required. Today's net is frequently wider than mine
- [ ] 4.5 m (5 yd) of 10 cm (4 in) wide cream cotton edging lace for frill at top
- [ ] 4 m (4½ yd) of 1.5 cm (½ in) wide cotton tape for stay stitching and tying to hoop
- [ ] 4 m (4½ yd) of 2.5 cm (1 in) wide cream satin ribbon for hanging ties
- [ ] One 45 cm (18 in) diameter wooden or bamboo hoop
- [ ] 1 reel Madeira Tanne 50 cream with bobbin to match
- [ ] Two pre-wound Madeira bobbins
- [ ] Pins, scissors, paper for stabilizer cut into 5 cm (2 in) wide strips, water fading pen.

PREPARATION

- [ ] Cut a 45 cm (18 in) diameter circle from a doubled piece of net and stitch together around edges with cotton tape to strengthen the seam.
- [ ] Cut net into three 4 m (4½ yd) lengths, join together on an overlocker (serger) with a narrow rolled hem or use a narrow zig zag stitch to make a 4.12 m (4½ yd) width (see note page 74)
- [ ] Cut a strip 26 cm (10 in) wide from bottom of joined net. Attach cotton edging lace to right side of netting.

Mosquito Net

Today a mosquito net is more decorative than functional, but in the tropics it is a necessary item. You can purchase one relatively inexpensively from specialty shops, so you may choose to do this and dye it and decorate it to suit your bedroom scheme. My netting was manufactured before World War II and I bought it in a job lot along with yards of old silk ribbons.

METHOD

1. Using paper as a stabilizer, cream Tanne thread through the needle and pre-wound bobbin, embroider st. # 21 around the netting on all raw edges. Using a small, sharp pair of scissors, cut away excess fabric from around the scallops.
2. Place frill, right side of lace uppermost, over right side of netting at the top of the mosquito net, with raw edges together and gather to fit the circumference of the wooden hoop.
3. Join frill from the wrong side with a small seam.
Attach frill and net to the net circle as you would a frill to the front of a cushion, see page 25.
4. Cut tape into 50 cm (20 in) lengths. Fold in half and attach at six evenly spaced intervals around underside of the circle's circumference; this is to attach net circle to hoop top.
5. Cut cream satin ribbon into four equal lengths and attach to the outside of the net circle at four equal intervals. These ribbons tie together for hanging and balance the circle.
6. Iron netting, attach to the circular hoop from the underside by tying tapes to wooden hoop. Tie four ribbons together for hanging from above the bed. The look is romantic and whimsical. I just love it.

MATERIALS

- ☐ Purchased cream dust ruffle
- ☐ Cream netting. Casing is cut twice the depth of the dust ruffle frill. Calculate the amount required by adding twice the length of your mattress to one width and doubling it
- ☐ Velcro tape to go on two long sides, and one short side of dust ruffle
- ☐ 6 m (7 yd) white tape 1 cm (⅜ in) wide
- ☐ 1 reel Madeira Tanne 50 thread
- ☐ Bobbin to match the above thread.

NOTE

To join the net into one piece, I used my overlocker/serger set on a very narrow rolled hem. If you do not have an overlocker/serger then a narrow zigzag can roll and whip these seams.

Dust Ruffle

To save time (I'm always in a rush) I purchased a cream dust ruffle and added a gathered casing of net to its two sides and end. Silk flowers are placed inside the casing for a uniquely romantic effect. The casing is closed with Velcro so it can be pulled apart and the flowers removed for washing. Not only is this a beautiful furnishing concept, but it is practical as well. Again I used my wonderful old netting.

METHOD

1. Join netting into a continual strip that in total is double the sum of twice the length and one width of your mattress.
2. Gather up one long side of netting to match the frill on the purchased dust ruffle. Stitch in place over the seam of the frill of the dust ruffle, right sides together.
3. Stitch the Velcro tape (loop side) over the top of one long side of the net frill seam with the loop side of the Velcro facing uppermost.
4. Gather up the other long side of the net frill to match the first. Attach 1 cm (⅜ in) cotton tape along the gathers on the other edge of net strip but on the other side (this is the right side). Attach Velcro tape (hook side) to the wrong side of the net strip along the gathers with the hook side uppermost.
5. The net strip folds back up on itself to form a casing and the Velcro tape holds it in place.

Arsenic and Old Lace Vest

Because it is a small project,
requires no fitting or tailoring but is
very eye-catching and glamorous this
vest is always a firm favourite at
demonstrations and craft shows.
When explaining its construction
and decoration I've heard the words
'love that vest technique' so often that
they have become its catch phrase.
Again it is only calico with layered
ribbon, doilies, hand dyed laces
and machine embroidery. Believe me it
takes no time at all to make. And best of
all, the finished article can be worn
with almost everything and it
also makes a great gift.

NOTE

Don't be fooled by the elaborate look of this vest – the embellishments
and construction are surprisingly simple. Much of the success of its design
lies in the accurate matching of the ribbon, lace and fabric pieces on the
fronts; they are mirror images of one another.

MATERIALS

- ☐ Purchased vest pattern (I used McCalls 7407 because it is so easy)
- ☐ 1 m (40 in) unbleached calico (muslin)
- ☐ 1 m (40 in) coffee coloured lining fabric
- ☐ 10 cm (4 in) apricot fabric for applique
- ☐ 1 m (40 in) Pellon
- ☐ 50 cm (20 in) Vliesofix/Wonderunder
- ☐ 4 m (4½ yd) narrow apricot satin piping
- ☐ 46 cm (18 in) apricot satin ribbon 5 cm (2 in) wide
- ☐ 62 cm (24 in) coffee satin ribbon 5 cm (2 in) wide
- ☐ 62 cm (24 in) cotton edging lace 10 cm (4 in) wide
- ☐ Doily 12 cm (5 in) diameter
- ☐ Hand dyed lace pieces from Judith and Kathryn
- ☐ Battenburg lace doily 20 cm (8 in) diameter in cream for centre back
- ☐ Large hand dyed lace triangular shape from Judith and Kathryn
- ☐ Threads as per *Arsenic and Old Lace* colours (see page 18) including Madeira Monofil
- ☐ One reel cream Madeira Tanne 50 construction thread
- ☐ Matching bobbin for above thread
- ☐ Two dusty pink tassels
- ☐ Blue water fading pen, ruler, pins, scissors.

PREPARATION

- ☐ Iron Pellon to back of calico. Cut out pattern of vest in Pellon backed calico. Make darts on the lower edge of back, press flat and topstitch from the right side on both sides of each dart. Cut out lining from lining fabric.
- ☐ Iron Vliesofix to the back of all ribbon, lace, apricot fabric for applique and doily pieces.
- ☐ Cut small doily in half, and ribbon and edging lace in half widthwise.
- ☐ On both front pieces mark a point on the side just under the arm and another 20 cm (8 in) from the bottom point and draw a line between these two points.
- ☐ Pin lower edge of coffee ribbon on this line. Pin straight edge of lace just under coffee ribbon. Pin apricot ribbon on top of coffee ribbon, with straight side of half doily under apricot ribbon.
- ☐ Ensure all fabric, lace and ribbon pieces match on centre front of vest and iron in place.
- ☐ Place hand dyed lace pieces over lace edging and onto coffee ribbon, angled as in the photograph from front edge towards underarm, and iron in place.
- ☐ Iron Battenburg lace doily in place, centring it on the back of the vest between the two arm holes.
- ☐ Iron triangular lace piece in centre back lining up with bottom edge of vest and overlapping Battenburg doily.

METHOD

Set machine up for free motion embroidery, straight stitch and monofilament thread. Stitch down all doily and lace pieces, following the doily shape.

FRONTS AND BACK

1. Draw in bow loops on left hand side of doily vest back, with tails beneath the doily on the bottom right hand corner. Use bow pattern from Pillow Sham on page 71.
2. Draw one bow loop on each side of both fronts above the top of the half doily.
3. Draw one ribbon tail exiting from beneath edging lace to the side of the lace motif.
4. Stitch all inside edges of bow loops and tails on fronts and back of vest with thread 1082 and st. # 6 and outside edges with thread 1060 st. # 14.

VEST FRONTS EMBROIDERY

1. On outside edge of edging lace thread 1060, st. # 15. Use same thread st. # 4 on the outside edge of half doilies.

2. Applique apricot ribbon with thread 1053 st. # 11 then do the outside edge with same thread in st. # 23.

3. Applique bottom of coffee ribbon with 1055 st. # 4, then applique outside edge on lace with same thread, st. # 13.

4. Embroider a flower motif on the bow loop and two butterflies overlapping on apricot ribbon.

5. Using lily applique design/motif (see page 25) and apricot fabric embroider lily motif facing down on coffee ribbon with thread 1060. With same thread embroider st. # 13 around outside edge of applique.

6. Repeat for both fronts, flopping the sequence to make a mirror image of the overall design for the other side. Trim all excess threads and stabilizer, press and put to one side.

VEST BACK EMBROIDERY

1. Using the same thread colours as for the front, embroider seven butterflies at random (three on left of doily, two to the top right of doily, two at bottom right over ribbon tails and one bottom left).

2. Using the detail photograph of the back as a guide, embroider a flower motif on the bottom left in 1053 apricot and 1060 silver grey and beside it a lily in apricot.

3. Use the silver grey and apricot for another flower motif in centre of doily on back.

Above: Detail of the vest fronts showing how most of the design elements mirror each other on both sides with a little variation in embroidery at the top.
Left: Back view of the vest.

FINISHING

1. Join shoulder seams, and top stitch from the right side flat.

2. Attach piping around armholes. Join side seams, again top stitch from the right side.

3. Attach piping around outside edge of vest, catching tassels on two front points. Pin tassels to inside of vest until lined.

4. Join shoulder and side seams of vest lining. Pin lining to vest making sure it fits well. Pin around armholes, but do not sew. Attach lining to vest around all outside edges, leaving a 20 cm (8 in) opening in centre back for turning.

5. Clip all seams, remove pins around armholes, turn to right side and slip stitch opening closed. Turn under 20 cm (8 in) opening and pin. Turn under lining around armholes, slipstitch.

6. Press vest with a good steam iron. Top stitch around all sides of vest and armholes 3 mm (⅛ in) from piping.

MATERIALS

- [ ] 30.5 cm (12 in) unbleached calico (muslin)
- [ ] 1 m (40 in) Pellon
- [ ] 50 cm (20 in) floral fabric in several grey green and apricot shades
- [ ] 50 cm (20 in) apricot pink silk dupion
- [ ] 60 cm (24 in) backing fabric
- [ ] 2.15 m (2⅓ yd) grey green insertion braid piping
- [ ] Robin silk print from Judith and Kathryn
- [ ] 2 m (80 in) coffee coloured leafy lace
- [ ] 6 large silk ribbon roses (apricot)
- [ ] Small silk ribbon roses (apricot and dusty pink)
- [ ] 3 bow charms that have been antiqued with black paint
- [ ] 5 m (5½ yd) of 4 cm (1½ in) wide grey green organza ribbon
- [ ] 4 m (4½ yd) of 2.5 cm (1 in) wide apricot organza ribbon
- [ ] Threads: use the full list of *Arsenic and Old Lace* colours (see page 18) plus gold metallic # 7 and Rayon 40 in 1341 and 1385
- [ ] 1 reel Madeira Tanne 50 in cream
- [ ] Matching bobbin for the above thread
- [ ] 1 reel Madeira Monofil
- [ ] Madeira pre-wound bobbin
- [ ] Pins, scissors, ruler, rotary cutter and mat, blue water marking pen, tape measure, quilting ruler.

Romantic Wall Hanging

I have always loved hand embroidery and did it for years. Now I have to turn to other methods to achieve similar effects because of aches and pains in my hands. This wall hanging combines a lovely silk print with lace, organza ribbons, charms, an original bread dough vase, machine embroidery and silk ribbon roses. Although the result is not quite hand embroidery, the feeling and richness of the piece is very close indeed.

PREPARATION

- [ ] Cut a piece of Stick-it-all stabilizer and put it on the back of the silk print.
- [ ] Cut a piece of Pellon to fit the above silk print – put aside.
- [ ] Cut calico and Pellon 51 cm × 30.5 cm (20 in × 12 in), iron Pellon to back of calico.
- [ ] Cut one piece of Pellon 61 cm × 41 cm (24 in × 16 in) and floral fabric the same size. Iron Pellon to back of floral fabric.
- [ ] Cut two 62 cm × 10 cm (24½ in × 4 in) and two 56 cm × 10 cm (22 in × 4 in)

strips of apricot silk dupion for sashing strips. Also cut same quantity and size of Pellon and iron these to back of sashing strips.

- [ ] Cut quilt binding strips of apricot silk dupion on the straight: two 10 cm × 80 cm (4 in × 32 in) and two 58 cm × 10 cm (23 in × 4 in). Fold strips in half lengthwise and iron.
- [ ] Cut 2.5 cm (1 in) strips of Vliesofix, iron them to the folded edge of the binding strips, leave paper in tact.

METHOD

SILK PRINT

1. Using free motion embroidery, straight stitch and matching threads to the picture, highlight the red breasts of the robins and some of the apple blossoms.

2. Using gold thread and st. # 13 embroider around the frame in the silk print with scallops facing into the centre.

3. Using the same gold thread and st. # 14 stitch around the outside edge of the previous row of scallop stitches.

4. Place silk print in the embroidery hoop and embroider a flower cluster in the centre of the frame using the above listed threads. Embroider three small floral sprays; one in top left of frame and two in bottom right corner of frame.

5. Lower feed dogs again and free motion stipple with gold thread around floral spray.

Detail of the ribbon work and embroidery on the silk print centre block of the wall hanging.

6. Remove stabilizer from back of silk print and iron Pellon to the back of print. Press with an applique mat, trim off excess from around the edge.

ADDING CALICO BLOCK

1. Fold under a narrow hem on the silk print and top stitch it to Pellon-backed calico block.

2. Cut length of lace in half; lace will be flopped on one side of the silk print to give a mirror reverse effect around its edge. Iron Vliesofix to the backs of both pieces of edging lace. Pin lace around the silk print so that the long curve of the leaf just sits on the edge of the print and the feathered leaf edges face out. Shape lace up to a peak at the top and down to a smaller one at the bottom. Iron lightly in place.

3. Take organza ribbon and, starting at the top on one side, thread it through the lace (you will be able to ease the lace away where necessary) ruching it up as you go, and pin in place. Adjust ruches to your satisfaction and ensure that the ends of the ribbon (at the top) are fairly equal in length.

4. Thread machine with monofilament thread, large free motion foot (for a clear view) and free motion the lace down, catching the ribbon in place at the same time. Use a small pair of overlocking/serger tweezers to ease the ribbon gently in place. Finish ends off with a bow at the top of the lace.

5. Take apricot organza ribbon and fill in the calico spaces at the top and bottom of the silk print, ruching up as you go.

ADDING THE FLORAL PIECE

1. Curve corners of calico rectangle and centre in Pellon backed floral fabric piece. Stitch calico down onto the above, close to

the edge. Press all pieces, being careful not to flatten ribbon.

2. Stitch green insertion braid piping around the outside edge of the floral fabric, top and bottom first and then the sides.

SASHING PIECES

1. Stitch apricot silk dupion sashing pieces to the outside edge of floral fabric trimmed with piping, sides first and then the top and bottom.

2. Enlarge bow loops and tails pattern (see overleaf) and draw in the top right hand corner of the apricot sashing. Embroider outline with thread colour 1082 and st. # 4. Define the ribbon folds with free motion shading in the same coloured thread.

3. Embroider five sprays of flowers in soft apricot and cream threads on the bottom left and right corners, along the bottom and up the left side.

4. Embroider small one tone butterflies in thread colours 1054 and 1084; three in the top left corner, four on the ribbon tails, two on the left hand side sashing and three among the floral sprays.

FURTHER EMBROIDERY

1. Using the same butterfly motif, embroider three on the bottom of the calico block and one on each side of the green organza bow, to hold ribbon tails in place.

2. Applique calico to floral fabric, around the edge with thread 1306 and st. # 13. Outside this row of stitching work with the same thread and st. # 15 onto the floral fabric.

BACKING THE HANGING

Apply wall hanging backing, bonding with powder as explained on page 13.

Thread machine with monofilament thread, large free motion foot (for a clear view) and free motion the lace down, catching ribbon in place at the same time.

To attach the silk roses, take off the machine foot, lower feed dogs, use monofilament thread and stitch through the centre with several straight stitches.

OUTLINE AND STIPPLE QUILTING

1. Using monofilament thread and free motion stitching outline quilt around the centre silk print and lace edges. Outline quilt the centre calico block as well as all the floral sprays, butterflies and bow loops and tails.
2. Change to thread 1306 and stipple quilt the floral fabric border.

MAKING HANGERS AND BINDING

Make hangers for the top edge of the hanging and pin them in place. Apply binding as explained in the straight binding technique on page 14. Press down on the back.

TO FINISH

1. Finish off your work of art by stitching on the silk roses. To do this I took the foot off my machine, lowered feed dogs, used monofilament thread and stitched the roses down through the centre with several straight stitches. If your roses look too uniform in colour use a little blusher on a make up brush and give them a blush in the centre. Another trick to take the new look out of rose colour is to make up a strong tea/coffee dye (see page 17) and dab it on their petal tips with a cotton tip.
2. To 'antique' the charms, just brush in a little acrylic black paint and quickly wipe the excess away so that the black paint stays in the crevices.
3. Glue or stitch the charms in place. Sign and date you work of art and wait for the reaction from family and friends.

**WALL HANGING
BOW AND SWAG**
Enlarge by 200%.

Sources and Suppliers

Published by Aussie Publishers 25 Izett Street, Prahran, Victoria 3181, Australia
Tel: +61-3-9529 4400 Fax +61-3-9525 1172
Email:penguin@netspace.net.au
Website: http://www.penguin-threads.com.au

BOOKS

Gary Clarke
☐ Embroidery and Candlewicking Designs
☐ Cats: Inspiration for Needlework
☐ Bouquets, Bows and Bugs
☐ Candlewicking and Beyond
☐ Simply Flowers

Stewart Merrett
☐ Appliqué Art   ☐ Appliqué Alphabet
☐ Cross Stitch Pack

Jenny Haskins
☐ Amadeus   ☐ Machine Embroidery

Judy Thomson
☐ Heirloom Timepiece

Anne van der Kley
☐ Serging Australia

VIDEOS

Jenny Haskins
☐ A Touch of Class – Sewing with Metallic Threads   ☐ Over the Top – Decorative Overlocking/Serging

Leisa Pownall
☐ The A to Z of Hand Embroidery
☐ More Embroidery Stitches and Shadow Embroidery
☐ Animals & Flowers in Bullion Stitch
☐ The Wonderful World of Smocking

Eileen Campbell
☐ Machine Appliqué
☐ Basic Free Machine Embroidery
☐ An Introduction to Machine Quilting

Nola Fossey
☐ Creating Wearable Art

Gabriella Verstraeten
☐ Having Fun with Machine Embroidery
☐ Appliqué with a Difference

EMBROIDERY THREADS

Madeira Australia
25 Izett Street Prahran, VIC 3181, Australia
Tel: +61-3-9529 4400   Fax +61-3-9525 1172
Email:penguin@netspace.net.au

Walker Textile Ltd
23 Fairfax Avenue, Penrose, Auckland
New Zealand
Tel: 0-9-579 0009   Fax: 0-9-579 5700

S.C.S. Madeira USA
9631 NE Colfax Street, Portland, Oregon
97220 USA Tel: 800-547-8025/503-252-1452 Fax: 503-252-7280
Email: scs@madeirathreads.com

Madeira Threads (UK) Limited
York Road, Thirsk,
North Yorkshire YO7 3BX UK
Tel: 01845 524880 Fax: 01845 525046
Email: acts@madeira.co.uk

Judith and Kathryn
Silk prints and hand dyed laces.
Fax/tel: 61 8 8276 8689 Tel: 61 8 8271 2238
Email: sjcoombe@senet.com.au
US supplier, see Australian Publications

Freudenberg P/L
Suppliers of Pellon, Vliesofix/Wonderunder
Tel: 61 3 9464 1022 Fax: 61 3 9464 0394

Australian Publications
3010 W. Anderson Lane, Suite G
Austin, Texas 78757 USA Tel: 1 888 788 6572
Fax: 512 452 3196 Email: sewmor@aol.com

Jenny Haskins Email: jenny@rpi.net.au

Acknowledgements

I would like to thank some exceptional people who made this book possible.

To the Giver of creativity – for my many gifts.

To my beautiful, loving, accepting daughter, Sam, who is my calm
through all storms and is so wise. I love you.

My first born, elder son, Jason, who survived my
mistakes. You have so much to offer this world. Have a great
life and thank you for being part of mine.

I wouldn't be without my parents, Ron and Mary Gray,
who celebrate 60 years of marriage this year. You are amazing people
and touch the lives of all who pass your way.

Judith and Kathryn of the business of the same name are
both amazing ladies who are part of my creativity. Their wonderful
colours in lace and pictures inspire me. Thank you for your
giving ways and quiet strength.

Diane and Simon, the patient photographer and design artists behind
the scenes. Your standard of excellence speaks for itself.

Michael Sput of Penguin Threads and Aussie Publishers for
having the vision and faith in Australian artists.

To Pfaff sewing machines who gave me the chance to explore
a whole new dimension in my life and gave me the strength to follow
a dream – you will always be part of me.

Index